Working With
Sample Data

Working With Sample Data

Exploration and Inference

Priscilla Chaffe-Stengel
California State University, Fresno

Donald N. Stengel
California State University, Fresno

First published in 2011 by
Business Expert Press, LLC
222 East 46th Street, New York, NY 10017
www.businessexpertpress.com

ISBN-13: 978-1-60649-213-0 (paperback)

ISBN-13: 978-1-60649-214-7 (e-book)

DOI 10.4128/978160649214

A publication in the Business Expert Press Quantitative Approaches to Decision Making collection

Collection ISSN (print): Forthcoming
Collection ISSN (electronic): Forthcoming

Cover design by Jonathan Pennell
Interior design by Scribe Inc.

First edition: June 2011

10 9 8 7 6 5 4 3 2 1

Printed in the United States of America.

Abstract

Managers and analysts routinely collect and examine key performance measures to better understand their operations and make good decisions. Being able to render the complexity of operations data into a coherent account of significant events requires an understanding of how to work well with raw data and to make appropriate inferences.

Although some statistical techniques for analyzing data and making inferences are sophisticated and require specialized expertise, there are methods that are understandable and applicable by anyone with basic algebra skills and the support of a spreadsheet package. By applying these fundamental methods themselves rather than turning over both the data and the responsibility for analysis and interpretation to an expert, managers will develop a richer understanding and potentially gain better control over their environment. This text is intended to describe these fundamental statistical techniques to managers, data analysts, and students.

Statistical analysis of sample data is enhanced by the use of computers. Spreadsheet software is well suited for the methods discussed in this text. Examples in the text detail for the reader how to apply Microsoft Excel.

Keywords

Statistics, sample data, sampling, data analysis, descriptive statistics, statistical inference, hypothesis testing

Contents

About the Authors

Priscilla Chaffe-Stengel

Priscilla Chaffe-Stengel is a Professor of Information Systems and Decision Sciences at California State University, Fresno. She received a PhD in Design and Evaluation of Educational Programs and an Educational Specialist Degree in Program Evaluation from Stanford University, as well as an MA in Mathematics from California State University, Fresno. Dr. Chaffe-Stengel has a wide range of experience teaching mathematics and statistics, ranging from junior high school to graduate-level courses.

Dr. Chaffe-Stengel has taught statistical analysis, quantitative analysis, and sampling at the university level. She coordinates the quantitative and statistical analysis courses in the Craig School of Business and teaches in both the MBA Program and Executive MBA Program. She has served the university and the school as assessment coordinator and as the Faculty Fellow in Institutional Research and Assessment. She has published articles in *For the Learning of Mathematics*, the *Journal of Foodservice Business Research*, the *Journal of Modelling in Management*, and the *Journal of Cooperative Education and Internships*. She has also created supplementary materials for several business statistics textbooks.

Donald N. Stengel

Donald N. Stengel is a Professor and Chair of the Department of Information Systems and Decision Sciences at California State University, Fresno. Previously he served as the Director of the MBA Program at California State University, Fresno. He received a PhD in Engineering-Economic Systems from Stanford University. Prior to joining the faculty at California State University, Fresno, Dr. Stengel worked for eight years as a management consultant developing planning models for agriculture and energy.

Dr. Stengel has taught managerial economics, business forecasting, statistics, and quantitative methods. He teaches in both the MBA Program and Executive MBA Program. He is a member of the National Association for Business Economics, the Institute for Operations Research and Management Science, and the American Statistical Association.

CHAPTER 1

Depicting Data in Telling Ways

Data flow from the pulse of business: your operations, your business, your market, your industry. Managers and analysts routinely collect and examine key performance measures to better understand their operations and make good decisions. Statistics is the study of principles and methods for exploring data and making correct conclusions.

Developing a full and articulated understanding of key performance measures often begins with a descriptive summary. Descriptive summaries can be developed graphically, which we address here, or numerically, which we develop in the next chapter.

Descriptive Narration

Graphic summaries provide a picture of key data that can be used to elicit important questions, fuel understanding, and facilitate communication. Important data tell stories worth listening to and worthy of retelling. Good graphics capture the detail in the data as well as the overview of their story. They arise in complex environments, so their summaries should depict their complexity. Good graphics present the actual data and show causality, multiple comparisons, multiple perspectives, the effects of the processes that lead to their creation, or the effects of subsequent changes made to those processes. They should visually reinforce the reason the data are of significance and integrate number, word, and illustration.

Complexity is difficult to display, for obvious reasons. Still, complexity can be thoughtfully captured in sequenced layers that allow the content to unfold, inviting interpretation and developing their meaning in the process. A rich and insightful discussion of graphic excellence

can be found in any of the works by Edward Tufte (http://www
.edwardtufte.com).

Data are generated either by counts or by measurements. Count data
arise in settings where sampled elements are classified by a key attribute
and assigned to categories, such as defective versus acceptable products,
commodities whose prices rose as opposed to remained the same or even
fell, or the number of sales made using credit rather than debit card,
check, or cash. These are qualitative, or categorical, variables and their
summaries are handled differently from quantitative variables. Quantitative variables capture data arising from measurements that include the
dimensions of time, distance, length, volume, rates, percent, and mone-
tary value. Some qualitative sample data can, under certain circumstances,
be converted to rates or percents and can then be treated as quantitative
sample data. Also, quantitative data can be assigned to intervals of measurement values that serve as categories and can be treated using methods
appropriate to qualitative data.

Summarizing Qualitative Variables

Qualitative variables can answer the question: how many or how frequently? Qualitative sample data are discrete counts of elements in
separate categories. Some qualitative variables may have only two categories (for example, defective or acceptable) or have multiple categories (for
example, numbers of sales by geographic region within the service area).

Summarizing sample data for qualitative variables by category can
be achieved in a column chart, where the horizontal axis marks each
category and a column rises over the category to a level marked on the
vertical axis by the count of elements in each category. Columns in the
graph do not touch across the categories to convey the fact that there is
not an implied continuum or even necessarily an order in which the categories are listed across the horizontal axis. See Figure 1.1 for an example
of a column chart for the number of nonfatal occupational injuries and
illnesses involving day(s) away from work in 2008 as reported by the U.S.
Bureau of Labor Statistics.

While the data reported in Figure 1.1 are accurate, they are one
dimensional. They do not invite insight, comparison, or perspective. The

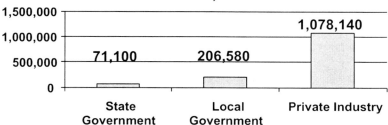

Figure 1.1. An Example of a **Column** Chart: *Number of Injuries and Illnesses in the United States in 2008 (http://www.bls.gov/news .release/osh2.t01.htm)*

data would be more telling if presented as an incidence rate on a common basis. See Figure 1.2.

Even though the data reported in Figure 1.2 are also one dimensional, they are reported as a rate applied to a common basis of 10,000 workers, which invites comparison and some insight.

Sometimes data can be split on an additional dimension and summarized in a stacked or side-by-side column chart, as shown in Figures 1.3 and 1.4.

The introduction of an additional dimension leads us to recognize the low numbers of injuries and illnesses reported among workers producing

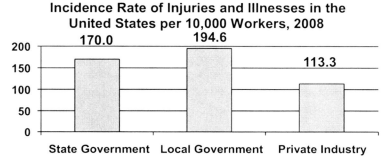

Figure 1.2. An Example of a **Column** Chart: *Incidence Rate of Injuries and Illnesses in the United States per 10,000 Workers in 2008 (http://www.bls.gov/news.release/osh2.t01.htm)*

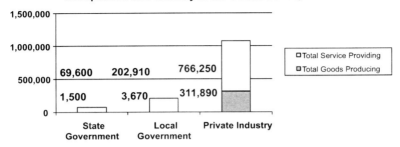

Figure 1.3. An Example of a **Stacked Column Chart,** *Comparison of the Numbers of Injuries and Illnesses by Occupations and Industry in the United States, 2008 (http://www.bls.gov/news.release/osh2 .t01.htm)*

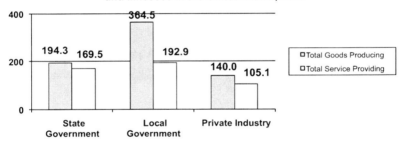

Figure 1.4. An Example of a **Side-by-Side Column Chart,** *Comparative Incidence Rates per 10,000 Workers for Injuries and Illnesses in the United States, 2008 (http://www.bls.gov/news.release/osh2.t01.htm)*

goods in the state and local government sectors. Given state and local government workers are largely in the services sector, however, these results are not terribly surprising.

With the conversion of data to a comparable basis per 10,000 workers shown in Figure 1.4, the introduction of the second dimension of occupation generates an interesting insight—that workers in the goods producing occupations within local governments registered an injury/illness incidence rate

1. 88% higher than workers in comparable occupations within state governments:

   Rate of injury/illness, goods producing, local versus state government $= \dfrac{364.5}{194.3} = 1.876$ or approximately 88% higher in local government than state government, and

2. 160% higher than workers in comparable occupations within private industry:

   Rate of injury/illness, goods producing, local government versus private industry $= \dfrac{364.5}{140} = 2.604$ or approximately 160% higher in local government than private industry.

We can also see that workers in service-providing occupations within private industry were significantly less injury/illness prone than in either governmental sectors. The magnitudes of differences reported in the graphic give readers pause to consider a number of questions: possible differences in the nature of jobs among the different sectors, the possibility of different training for worker safety and health, the impact of potentially differing benefit packages, among others. Underscored here is an important principle of data summary: When surprises occur, say so, and present the surprising results as clearly as possible. If the magnitudes of results are unexpected, as they are in this case, say so, and present the surprising magnitudes as clearly as possible. If no data occur in an expected category, say so, and discuss what the results might mean.

A special note of caution is due in working with the data shown in Figure 1.4. Because there are comparatively fewer workers in goods producing within governmental sectors, the incidence rates across service providing and goods producing occupations are not additive within sectors. We would have to convert the rates to an average weighted by the number of workers in each occupation within each sector to achieve additive rates. The caution echoes a broader principle in graphical integrity to avoid distortion of the data.

Summarizing Quantitative Variables

Where qualitative variables respond to the question of how many, quantitative variables can answer the question of how much. Sample data generated by measurements can take on any value along a number line and are considered continuous, in comparison to count data, which are discrete because they take on only the whole number counts of sampled elements.

Comparable to using the column chart for categorical data, summary of continuous variables can be accomplished with the creation of classes into which the various sample values can be sorted and counted. The resulting frequency distribution looks very much like a column chart, where the height of each column represents the counts of data in each class. In contrast to the column chart, however, columns in a frequency distribution are contiguous to convey the fact that there is a continuous scale on the horizontal axis. See Figure 1.5 for an example of a frequency distribution for the miles per gallon (MPG) ratings for city driving for subcompact cars, model year 2011, available for new car sales in the United States.

Information contained in the frequency distribution can also be displayed in a line graph, where the data point for the frequency is located at the center of each class interval. This is also referred to as a frequency polygon. See Figure 1.6.

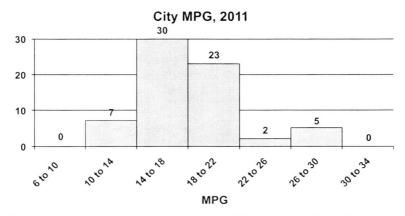

*Figure 1.5. An Example of a **Frequency Distribution**, U.S. City Driving MPG, Model Year 2011 (http://www.fueleconomy.gov)*

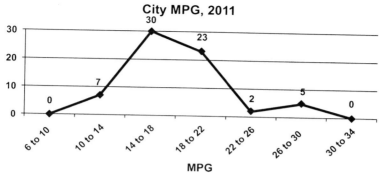

Figure 1.6. *An Example of a* **Line Graph**, *U.S. City Driving MPG, Model Year 2011 (http://www.fueleconomy.gov)*

When the message to convey is not the number of vehicles in each class but the comparative frequency of vehicles in each class, the use of a pie chart focuses the reader's eye on the portion of the total each class represents. A pie chart is a circular illustration of the total sample that is then broken into slices representing each class's relative frequency as a portion of the whole sample. See Figure 1.7. A pie chart can be used with quantitative data, as shown here, or with qualitative data, where slices represent the categories used to summarize the data.

City MPG, 2011

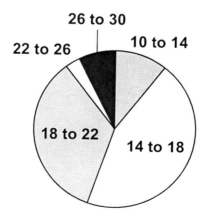

Figure 1.7. *An Example of a* **Pie Chart**, *U.S. City Driving MPG, Model Year 2011 (http://www.fueleconomy.gov)*

An interesting combination of column and line graph can be created as a Pareto chart depicting both frequency and cumulative relative frequency for each class. See Figure 1.8. Pareto charts can also be used with categorical data, when categories represented are given in decreasing order of incidence from left to right on the horizontal axis.

Bivariate Data

To investigate underlying relationships between measures, x-y scatterplots are useful in giving the reader a bird's eye view of potential relationships, where the horizontal x-axis represents the independent variable and the vertical y-axis represents the dependent variable. We can explore the relationship between, for example, the city mileage and the highway mileage for subcompact model cars for 2011. See Figure 1.9. The graph clearly shows the direct relationship between city and highway mileages. As a car's city mileage improves, so does its highway mileage.

The use of an x-y scatterplot is especially valuable in looking at potential causal relationships. Figure 1.10 depicts the city mileage as a function of, or effect of, the engine size for subcompact cars model year 2011. The graph strengthens the statement that increases in engine size cause decreases in the overall city mileage for the car.

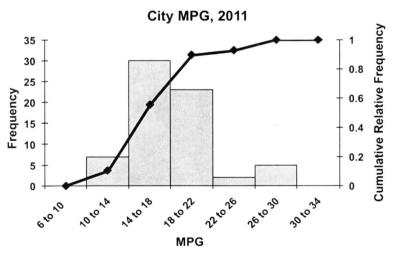

Figure 1.8. An Example of a **Pareto Chart**, *U.S. City Driving MPG, Model Year 2011 (http://www.fueleconomy.gov)*

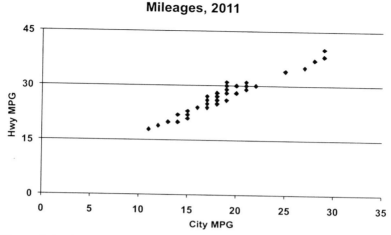

Figure 1.9. An Example of an x-y Scatterplot, Mileages for Subcompact Model Cars, 2011 (http://www.fueleconomy.gov)

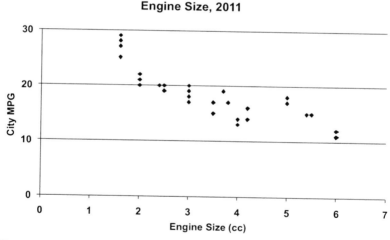

Figure 1.10. An Example of an x-y Scatterplot, Engine Size and City Mileage for Subcompact Model Cars, 2011 (http://www.fueleconomy.gov)

Gathering Data: Probabilistic Sampling Techniques

Collecting key performance data may present a challenge depending on the nature and complexity of underlying processes. Statistical inference requires careful data collection. Four sampling designs are reviewed here.

Simple Random Samples

When elements to be sampled occur in finite batches or cohorts and an ordered listing of them, or *sample frame*, is possible, a simple random sample is a straightforward technique to use in obtaining a random sample. In a simple random sample, every element in the population has an equal chance of being sampled. One means of constructing a random sample to assign a random number to each element in the sample frame, using either a random number table or Excel's built-in random number generator. A serial sort of the list based on the assigned random numbers identifies the order in which elements in the sample frame are selected.

For a qualitative variable, a minimum sample of 5% of the batch is usually required. When the batch or cohort is either very large or very small in size, a substantially different sample size may be in order. These considerations will be discussed in later sections. For a quantitative variable, a minimum sample of 30 elements is typically considered sufficient, although that number may be larger for variables over which measurement values differ greatly.

Systematic Samples

Sometimes sample elements occur in streams rather than batches, such as products off a manufacturing line, sales at an online site, or customers at a store site. Elements arrive sequentially rather than simultaneously, which precludes the creation of a sample frame since the elements to sample are not all present at once. To randomly sample from a stream of elements, a 1-in-k systematic sample may be used, where an initial element is randomly selected and then every k^{th} element is sampled. Systematic sampling is easy to use and has the advantage of sampling the population evenly. Caution must be used, however, if there is some preexisting pattern in the population of elements. A systematic sample is not an appropriate design to use in a population where some periodic pattern occurs because of the real possibility that sampled elements will themselves represent a cyclic bias in the measurement of interest and thereby distort the estimate of the true population measure. If a sample size and the population size are known, the period k within which to select the sampled element can be estimated by taking the population size and dividing by the desired sample size.

Stratified Samples

Where patterns do exist in the population being sampled, the population can be segmented into subpopulations with the use of nonoverlapping strata, or layers, of relatively similar elements. Every element in the population must be a member of one and only one subpopulation. A sampling design should be used so that variability on the measure of interest within each stratum is minimized, and variability between strata is maximized. Proportionate samples of each subpopulation should reflect the fractional representation of each stratum within the population. For example, if women represent 67% of the population and men the remaining 33%, the respective sample sizes taken should reflect the same proportions. Either simple random samples or systematic samples can then be selected from within each stratum so that elements within each layer have the same chance of being sampled. The resulting samples are then composed to form the total sample from the population. The use of a stratified sample forces the proportions of sampled elements to reflect the proportions of elements as they exist in the larger population and produce a reasonably precise and unbiased estimate of the variable being measured.

Cluster Samples

When a population can be divided into groups that are equally heterogeneous, with each group or cluster serving as a microcosm of the larger population, sampling a few randomly selected clusters can produce an unbiased estimate of the measure in the larger population. As with stratified sampling, the groupings, whether they are strata or clusters, must be mutually exclusive and collectively exhaustive. In cluster sampling, however, variability on the measure of interest is maximized within each cluster and minimized between clusters. By sampling within randomly selected clusters, the cost of data collection can be reduced, particularly when clusters are defined by geographic regions, allowing sampling to be done in a more narrowly defined geographic region.

The Focus of This Text

This text is about analyzing sample data. The techniques and examples used in this text assume the collection of simple random samples. For other sampling techniques, a more advanced sampling text should be consulted.

CHAPTER 2

Summarizing Location, Scatter, and Relative Position

Quantitative data can be described with numbers that summarize the center of a data set, the amount of scatter represented among its elements, and sometimes even the relative position of a particular value within the set of data. A distribution of quantitative data values can be characterized by its shape, its center, and its spread. Developing summary statistics is an important step in working with sample data.

Measures of Location

There are three measures of central tendency: the average value or mean, the middle value or median, and the most frequent value or mode. While the mode, by definition, is a member of the original set of data, the mean and the median do not necessarily belong to the original data set.

The Mean

The arithmetic average of a set of data is the mean. It is the sum of the individual data values divided by the number of observations. In the study and use of statistics, it is important to know whether the mean is formed using all elements in the population or whether the mean is based on a random sample of elements taken from the population. The population mean is denoted by the symbol μ, pronounced "*mew*," and the sample mean by the symbol $\bar{x}$. Their computations are the same, boxed for easy reference.

Population and Sample Means

$$\text{Population Mean: } \mu = \frac{\sum x_i}{N}$$

where x_i are all the data values in the population and N is the size of the population.

$$\text{Sample Mean: } \overline{x} = \frac{\sum x_i}{n}$$

where x_i are the data values randomly sampled and n is the sample size.

The mean is the most frequently used measure for the center of a set of data. The mean is sensitive to the presence of extreme values in a data set, however, and may not be a reliable measurement of the center of a distribution when outliers are present. Microsoft Excel can easily compute the mean for a set of sample data by typing into a spreadsheet cell the function =*average(range for data)*.

The Median

The middle value of an ordered set of data is the median.

- For an *odd* number of observations, the median is the middle number when the data are put in an ordered array.
- For an *even* number of observations, the median is the average of the middle two values when the data are put in an ordered array.

Unlike the mean, the value of the median is not influenced by the presence of outliers and may provide a more reliable estimate of a distribution's central value when outliers are present. In discussions of residential housing values, for example, we frequently see references to median home values in lieu of average home values because of the potential bias introduced by a few high-value homes into the calculation of the mean home value in a given market. Excel can easily compute the median for a set of sample data by typing into a spreadsheet cell the function =*median(range for data)*.

The Mode

The single most frequently occurring value in a data set is the mode. If there are two values that both occur with highest frequency observed in the data set, the data are said to be bimodal. It is possible that a mode does not exist in a data set. In general, the mode is not as reliable an estimate of the data set's central value, and so the mode is not used as often as the mean or the median to characterize the center of a distribution. Excel can easily compute the mode for a set of sample data by typing into a spreadsheet cell the function =*mode(range for data)*.

Comparing the Mean, the Median, and the Mode

A preliminary estimate of the shape of a distribution can be readily obtained using a comparison of the mean, the median, and the mode. If the value of the mean, the median, and the mode are all roughly equal, the shape of the distribution is said to be symmetric. If the mean is larger than the median and the mode, there are more values in the upper end of the distribution inflating the value of the mean. In that case, the distribution is skewed to the right, or positively skewed, with a longer tail into the right end of the distribution. If, on the other hand, the mean is smaller than the median or the mode, then there are more values in the lower end of the distribution pulling the value of the mean down. In that case, the distribution is skewed to the left, or negatively skewed, with a longer tail into the left end of the distribution. This is a valuable preliminary analysis to conduct, particularly on large data sets where it may be time consuming to build a frequency distribution to examine the shape graphically. With the use of Excel's built-in toolkit, descriptive summary statistics can be prepared easily, giving the analyst a sense of the shape of the distribution relatively quickly.

Estimating the Mean From Grouped Data

Sometimes managers may receive reports of data that have already been summarized into a frequency distribution. If the calculated mean is not included in the report, being able to back out an estimated mean is quite useful.

For estimating either the population or the sample mean from grouped data, we use the concept of a weighted average.

Estimated Mean From Grouped Data

$$\mu \text{ or } \bar{x} = \frac{\sum(\text{each class frequency} \cdot \text{its class midpoint})}{\text{the sum of the class frequencies}} = \frac{\sum f_i \cdot m_i}{n}$$

where f_i is the frequency for class i, m_i the midpoint for class i, and n the number of elements included.

Let's consider the example captured in Figure 1.5, Chapter 1, characterizing the city mileage for 67 subcompact cars. To estimate the mean, we set up the calculation as follows:

Class Interval	Midpoint	Frequency	Product
10 to 14	12	7	12 × 7 = 84
14 to 18	16	30	16 × 30 = 480
18 to 22	20	23	20 × 23 = 460
22 to 26	24	2	24 × 2 = 48
26 to 30	28	5	28 × 5 = 140
30 to 34	32	0	32 × 0 = 0
Sums		67	1212

So the estimate for the average city mileage for subcompact cars in model year 2011 is 1212 ÷ 67 or 18.09 miles per gallon (MPG). For comparison, the actual mean value for the 67 cars reported is 18.75 MPG.

Measures of Spread

In addition to determining the center of a distribution, describing the concentration of data around its center is important. We will cover three measures of spread or dispersion: the range, the variance, and the standard deviation.

The Range

A preliminary sense of the spread among data is given by the range over which the data vary, from the smallest value to the largest value in the data set. The range is technically defined as the difference between the maximum and the minimum values, although we often say that the data range from one value to the other, describing the range by stating the location of the two end points of the distribution. Because the range is established by the two extremes of the distribution, it is both the most sensitive of the measures of spread to the presence of outliers and the least representative of the dispersion among the complete set of data. Excel can easily compute the range for a set of sample data by typing into spreadsheet cells each of two functions

$$=max(range\ for\ data)$$
$$=min(range\ for\ data)$$

and then subtracting the minimum value from the maximum value.

The Variance

The variance is a frequently used measure of spread whose numerator is the sum of the squared differences of each value from its mean. When the population mean, μ, is known, the numerator is divided by the population size, N. The resulting measure is the population variance, σ^2, pronounced "*sigma-squared*." When the population mean is not known but is estimated by $\bar{x}$, the numerator is divided by the sample size minus one, $(n - 1)$. By dividing by one less than the sample size, we allow for more fluctuation in small samples. When samples are comparatively large, subtracting one from n does not make a significant impact on the overall value. The resulting measure is the sample variance, s^2.

Population and Sample Variance

Population Variance: $\sigma^2 = \dfrac{\Sigma(x_i - \mu)^2}{N}$

where x_i are all the data values in the population, μ is the population mean, and N is the size of the population.

Sample Variance: $s^2 = \dfrac{\Sigma\left(x_i - \bar{x}\right)^2}{n - 1}$

where x_i are the data values randomly sampled, $\bar{x}$ is the sample mean, and n is the sample size.

Excel can easily compute the variance for the set of population data by typing into a spreadsheet cell the function =varp(range for data) and can also compute the variance for the set of sample data by typing into a spreadsheet cell the function =var(range for data).

The Standard Deviation

The standard deviation is the positive square root of variance. For a population, the standard deviation is σ, or *sigma*, and for the sample, the standard deviation is *s*. Where the variance is given in squared units, the standard deviation is given in the same units the mean is reported in. So, if we are discussing the average value of a mutual fund in dollars, its variance is in squared dollars, but its standard deviation is in dollars, as the mean is reported. And that is a good part of its virtue.

A particularly useful expression of dispersion is given by the coefficient of variation, which is the standard deviation divided by the mean of the data set, written as a percent.

Coefficient of Variation

$$\textbf{For a population: } CV = \frac{\sigma}{\mu} \cdot 100$$

$$\textbf{For a sample: } CV = \frac{s}{\bar{x}} \cdot 100$$

In computing the coefficient of variation, we can compare the relative amount of dispersion across a number of sets of data, where the means and their standard deviations may be otherwise quite disparate. For example, coefficients of variation can be compared for "penny" stocks and for blue chip stocks, despite the fact that the mean value of "penny" stocks will be quite different from the mean value of the blue chip stocks. Making such comparisons yields measures of comparative risk or stability as a percent of the mean value of the stock. Excel can easily compute the standard deviation for a set of sample data by typing into a spreadsheet cell the function =stdev(range for data). Alternatively, if we have already computed the sample variance, we can simply take the square root of the sample variance by entering into a cell the equation =sqrt(variance). When calculating the standard deviation for a set of population data, the Excel formula is =stdevp(range for data).

Estimating the Standard Deviation From Grouped Data

If data have already been summarized into a frequency distribution and the standard deviation is not included in the report, being able to back out an estimated standard deviation is also useful.

For estimating either the population or the sample standard deviation from grouped data, we use the class frequencies, midpoints, and results of our prior calculations of the estimated mean.

Estimated Standard Deviation From Grouped Data

$$\text{For a population: } \sigma = \sqrt{\frac{\sum f_i \cdot m_i^2 - N \cdot \mu^2}{N}}$$

where f_i is the frequency for class i, m_i the midpoint for class i, μ is the estimated population mean, and N the number of elements in the population.

$$\text{For a sample: } s = \sqrt{\frac{\sum f_i \cdot m_i^2 - n \cdot \bar{x}^2}{n-1}}$$

where f_i is the frequency for class i, m_i the midpoint for class i, $\bar{x}$ is the estimated sample mean, and n the number of elements sampled.

Let's update the example characterizing the city mileage for 67 subcompact cars. Since there are no cars in the first and last categories, we eliminate those two lines to simplify the presentation here. To estimate the standard deviation, we set up the calculation as follows:

Class Interval	Midpoint	Frequency	f*m²
10 to 14	12	7	$7 \times 12^2 = 1008$
14 to 18	16	30	$30 \times 16^2 = 7680$
18 to 22	20	23	$23 \times 20^2 = 9200$
22 to 26	24	2	$2 \times 24^2 = 1152$
26 to 30	28	5	$5 \times 28^2 = 3920$
Sums		67	22960
Estimated sample mean		18.09	
		$n(x\text{-bar})^2 = 67 \times 18.09^2 = 21925.62$	
Estimated standard deviation $\sqrt{\dfrac{22960 - 21925.62}{67 - 1}} = 3.96$			

Since the units are in MPG, the sample standard deviation estimated from the group data is 3.96 MPG. For comparison, the actual standard deviation for the 67 cars reported is 3.71 MPG.

Chebyshev's Theorem and the Empirical Rule

Two applications using the mean and the standard deviation are given by Chebyshev's Theorem and the Empirical Rule. Chebyshev's Theorem is named after the Russian mathematician Pafnuty L'vovich Chebyshev who proved that a minimum percentage of data values fall within two bounds on either side of the mean. Stated specifically, Chebyshev proved that the minimum percentage of values lying within k ($k > 1$) units of standard deviation of the mean is given by the following formulation.

Chebyshev's Theorem

Regardless of the shape of distribution, the minimum percentage of values close to the mean is

$$\left(1 - \frac{1}{k^2}\right) \times 100$$

where k is the number of units of standard deviation from either a population or a sample.

This is true regardless of the shape of the underlying distribution. So, for example, we know that

- within $k = 1.25$ units of standard deviation, $\left(1 - \dfrac{1}{1.25^2}\right) \times 100$

  $= (0.36) \times 100 = 36\%$ or a minimum of 36% of all data values will fall within the interval $(\bar{x} - 1.25 \cdot s, \bar{x} + 1.25 \cdot s)$, and

- within $k = 1.5$ units of standard deviation $\left(1 - \dfrac{1}{1.5^2}\right) \times 100 +$

  $(0.556) \times 100 = 55.56\%$ or a minimum of 55.56% of all data values will fall within the interval $(\bar{x} - 1.5 \cdot s, \bar{x} + 1.5 \cdot s)$.

This can be a useful metric to anticipate the concentration of values close to the mean.

If the shape of the underlying distribution is known to be normal—that is, the distribution is bell-shaped and symmetric about the mean—then a stronger statement can be made than Chebyshev's Theorem provides us. If a distribution is normal, the Empirical Rule estimates a much more precise percentage of values that fall close to the mean. Again, the comparison of the mean, the median, and the mode can be useful in estimating the shape of the distribution.

The Empirical Rule

For normal distributions, the following is true:
- Approximately 68% of all data values will fall within one (1) unit of standard deviation of the mean.
- Approximately 95% of all data values will fall within two (2) units of standard deviation of the mean.
- Approximately 99% of all data values will fall within three (3) units of standard deviation of the mean.

Quantiles: Measures of Relative Position

A special class of measures is useful in dividing a data set into proportionate segments. They are quantiles, and we have already worked with one of them, the median.

- The *median* is a quantile that divides a data set into two equally populated halves, with 50% of the data set falling above the median and 50% of the data set falling below the median.
- A *quartile* divides a data set further by splitting the lower half and the upper half in two, so that there are four equally populated quarters of the data set, each containing 25% of the data values.
- A *decile* divides a data set into 10 equally populated segments, each containing 10% of the data values.
- A *percentile* divides a data set into 100 equally populated segments, each containing 1% of the data values.

If you have ever taken a national examination, you probably received a scaled score for the exam that was equated to a percentile. A reported score equated to the 87th percentile, for example, means that 87% of the people taking the same test earned scores at or below that reported score and 13% of the people taking the test earned scores at or above the reported score, which establishes a measure of the relative position of the reported score within the entire data set.

To identify a quantile, the data set must first be put in an ordered array, from smallest to largest value. While everyone agrees on the calculation procedure to find the median, differences in procedures can lead to small differences in the values given for other quantiles. One of the simplest procedures to find the first and third quartiles is to apply the procedure for finding the location of the median to the lower and upper halves of the data set. Applying it to the lower half yields the first quartile and applying it to the upper half yields the third quartile. To find the location of a particular percentile, A, for example, use the following procedure:

A Procedure to Find the Value of the Ath Percentile in a Data Set

1. Put the data set into an ordered array.
2. To find the location, L, at with A% of the data fall below that location, use the equation

$$L = \frac{A}{100} \cdot n$$

where L is the location in the data list at which A% of the data fall below it, and n is the number of data values in the list.

3. If L is not a whole number, the Ath percentile is the value in the data list located at the next largest whole number above L. If L is a whole number, the Ath percentile is the average of the two values in the data list located at the Lth position and at the $(L+1)^{st}$ position in the data list.

Excel can easily compute the kth quartile for a set of sample data by typing into a spreadsheet cell the function =*quart(range for data,k)* and can also easily compute the kth percentile for a set of sample data by typing into a spreadsheet cell the function =*percentile(range for data,k)*.

CHAPTER 3

Understanding the Normal Distribution and the *t*-Distribution

If you have ever watched someone sift flour in a kitchen or dig a hole and pile the dirt in the same place outside, you have seen a normal distribution, albeit somewhat imperfect. It is bell shaped, symmetric, peaked in the center with tails that trail off rapidly the greater the distance from the center. While imperfect versions of the normal distribution are easily seen in ordinary life, its discovery is credited to the great German mathematician Johann Carl Friedrich Gauss (1777–1855), who documented that errors of routine measurements often follow a normal distribution. Some normal distributions can be huge, as seen in a pile of hulls at the end of a dump chute from an almond hulling plant, for example, and others quite tiny in comparison. Normal distributions occur because the greatest numbers of elements in the "pile" fall straight down below the location of the end of the chute or the bottom of the sifter or the tip of the shovel. Some elements tumble off center, down the growing sides of the "pile." Unless otherwise constrained, occasionally an element will tumble relatively far away from the center. Because the height, μ, and breadth, σ, in different distributions can differ over many magnitudes, the standard normal distribution is introduced to standardize their discussion.

The Standard Normal Distribution

All normal distributions share the same shape, differing only by the location of the center and the degree of spread. The standard normal distribution is the normal distribution that has a mean of 0 and a standard deviation of 1. The axis along the bottom of the distribution represents the number of units of standard deviation a particular value is above or below its mean, which is called the z-score.

The standard normal distribution is useful because its table details the amount of area captured under the normal curve below a given value. The reason we care about the amount area captured under a normal curve is that it represents the likelihood that a value will fall within a defined segment of a normal distribution. Any normal distribution can be converted to the standard normal distribution by subtracting the value of its mean (or center point) and then dividing that difference by the standard deviation for the population. The Standard Normal Table converts the linear distance a value is away from its mean on the bottom axis of the distribution to the likelihood that a value will fall that far or less away from its mean, which is the area captured under the normal curve below that value. Let's investigate a few elementary examples.

Example 3.1.

What is the probability that a z-score will fall below a score of 1.04?

Answer

Locate the ones and tenths digits as a row header on the cumulative standard normal distribution. Locate the hundredths digit as a column header on the table and trace down the column and across the row identified to find their intersection. See Table 3.1. The answer is

$$P(z < 1.04) = 0.8508$$

Interpretation: Approximately 85.08% of the area under a normal curve will fall to the left of a z-score of 1.04. There is an approximate 85.08% chance that an element randomly selected from a normal population will fall below a z-score of 1.04.

Example 3.2.

What is the probability that a z-score will fall above a score of 1.04?

Answer

Using the same area found in Table 3.1, since we want the area above the given *z*-score, we subtract that area from 1. The answer is

$$1 - P(z < 1.04) = 1 - 0.8508 = 0.1492$$

Interpretation: Approximately 14.92% of the area under a normal curve will fall to the right of a *z*-score of 1.04. There is an approximate 14.92% chance that an element randomly selected from a normal population will fall above a *z*-score of 1.04.

Table 3.1. A Portion of the Cumulative Standard Normal Distribution Table

z	.00	.01	.02	.03	.04	.05	.06	.07	.08	.09
0.0	.5000	.5040	.5080	.5120	.5160	.5199	.5239	.5279	.5319	.5359
0.1	.5398	.5438	.5478	.5517	.5557	.5596	.5636	.5675	.5714	.5753
0.2	.5793	.5832	.5871	.5910	.5948	.5987	.6026	.6064	.6103	.6141
0.3	.6179	.6217	.6255	.6293	.6331	.6368	.6406	.6443	.6480	.6517
0.4	.6554	.6591	.6628	.6664	.6700	.6736	.6772	.6808	.6844	.6879
0.5	.6915	.6950	.6985	.7019	.7054	.7088	.7123	.7157	.7190	.7224
0.6	.7257	.7291	.7324	.7357	.7389	.7422	.7454	.7486	.7517	.7549
0.7	.7580	.7611	.7642	.7673	.7704	.7734	.7764	.7794	.7823	.7852
0.8	.7881	.7910	.7939	.7967	.7995	.8023	.8051	.8078	.8106	.8133
0.9	.8159	.8186	.8212	.8238	.8264	.8289	.8315	.8340	.8365	.8389
1.0	.8413	.8438	.8461	.8485	.8508	.8531	.8554	.8577	.8599	.8621
1.1	.8643	.8665	.8686	.8708	.8729	.8749	.8770	.8790	.8810	.8830

A special note is worth making at this point of our discussion. Sometimes we talk about *z*-scores that are strictly less than a given value, as we did in Example 3.1. Other times we talk about *z*-scores that are less than or equal to a given value. While the difference can be captured in notation mathematically,

$$P(z < 1.04) \text{ versus } P(z \le 1.04)$$

computationally there is no difference in the probability satisfying the two depictions. The reason is that a point has no breadth or depth. So an individual point, in this case $z = 1.04$, has no dimension and carries with it no area under the curve. You might recall that a geometric boundary that is excluded from an area is shown with a dotted line, and a boundary that is included in an area is shown with a solid line. But the inclusion of the single boundary point, and therefore its edge, makes no difference to the calculation of the area itself.

Standardizing Individual Data Values on a Normal Curve

Not all variables are normally distributed. Many events we can think of are skewed, like personal income or residential housing prices. However, if a variable is normally distributed, we can analyze its distribution through the standard normal distribution using the following equation:

Converting a Value to the Standard Normal Distribution

$$z = \frac{\text{a value} - \text{its mean}}{\text{its standard deviation}} = \frac{x - \mu}{\sigma}$$

where the z-score is the distance an individual value is away from its mean in terms of its standard deviation.

Let's consider an example.

Example 3.3.

Suppose we know that delivery times for an interstate package shipment company are known to be normally distributed with a mean of 3.5 days and a standard deviation of 0.8 days. What is the probability that a package will take more than 5 days to be delivered?

Answer

The individual package delivery time in question is 5 days, with a mean delivery time of $\mu = 3.5$ days and a standard deviation of $\sigma = 0.8$ days.

$$z = \frac{x - \mu}{\sigma} = \frac{5 - 3.5}{0.8} = 1.875 \approx 1.88$$

$$P(x > 5 \text{ days}) = P(z > 1.88) = 1 - 0.9699 = 0.0301$$

Interpretation: There is a slightly better than 3% chance that a package will require more than 5 days to be delivered by this company. While it is possible that a package will require more than 5 days to deliver, it is highly unlikely.

The *t*-Distribution

The Student's *t*-distribution, also known simply as the *t*-distribution, is bell-shaped, like the standard normal distribution. Like the standard normal distribution, the *t*-distribution also represents the distance a value is above or below its mean in terms of its standard deviation and converts that distance into the area under the curve beyond that value. In contrast, however, the *t*-distribution is less concentrated around the mean and has thicker tails than the *z*-distribution. In fact, the *t*-distribution is a family of curves that is flatter the smaller the sample size and that becomes more centrally mounded the larger the sample size. Fundamental to this dynamic is the notion of degrees of freedom (*df*), which is a measure of the strength of the sample in estimating the population mean. When estimating the value of a mean, we have $(n - 1)$ additional elements to support and refine the value of the first sampled element. Seen another way, once we know the mean of the sample, we only need to know $(n - 1)$ elements in the sample and the value of the remaining element is determined. So we have $(n - 1)$ degrees of freedom in the sample to estimate the mean.

Because the shape of the curve actually changes for each change in the degrees of freedom, a separate table for each *df* would be required to have the distribution fully displayed. To economize, the values for frequently used areas are extracted and displayed in a table for the *t*-distribution. Using the table for the *t*-distribution, then, requires we identify the degrees of freedom and the particular area of interest to find the *t*-coefficient, which is the number of units of standard deviation a value would be away from its mean in order to capture the desired area. To find the *t*-coefficient, for example, that marks off 10% of the area in the upper tail of the *t*-distribution for $df = 35$, we locate the column headed by $\alpha = 0.10$ and run across the row headed by $df = 35$ to find the value $t = 1.306$. An example, Example 3.4., will be developed later in the chapter using the *t*-distribution.

Understanding the Behavior of Sample Means

One of the main reasons we study samples from populations is because we want to estimate a population parameter like the mean. If we randomly gather one sample and compute its sample mean, and then randomly gather another sample and compute its sample mean, we will generally get different sample mean values. Further, it is highly unlikely any particular sample mean will be the true population mean, μ.

We take samples and infer back to what the samples say about the population they could have come from. In fact, if we took many samples and determined their sample means, the mean of all sample means taken from the population is the population mean itself: $\mu_{\bar{x}} = \mu$. The set of sample means for all possible samples of size n taken from a population defines a probability distribution referred to as the distribution of sample means or the sampling distribution of $\bar{x}$.

Error is inherent in the process of taking repeated samples. Inferences are, after all, based on incomplete data. The difference between the sample statistic and the population parameter it estimates is called the sampling error. We need to allow for error in our estimate of the population parameter. It can be shown mathematically that the standard deviation of the sampling distribution of the mean, *the standard error*, is given by $\sigma_{\bar{x}} = \sigma / \sqrt{n}$, where σ is the population standard deviation and n is the sample size.

Regardless of the sample size, the center of the sampling distribution of the mean is always the population mean: $\mu_{\bar{x}} = \mu$. Put another way, the center of the sampling distribution of the mean is not sensitive to the sample size. However, the standard deviation of the sampling distribution of the mean is sensitive to the sample size. The larger the sample size, n, the more similar the sample means will be and the more concentrated the sample means will be around the true population mean. In other words, the larger the sample size, the smaller the standard error and the more "peaked" or "mounded" the sampling distribution will be around the population mean; the smaller the sample size, the larger the standard error and the "flatter" or less concentrated the sampling distribution will be around the population mean.

When the Population Distribution Is Normal and σ Is Known

The sample size does not affect the location of the center of the sampling distribution, but it does affect the shape, the "moundedness," of the sampling distribution. The larger the sample size, the more concentrated, the more "mounded," the sampling distribution of the mean becomes. How mounded the sampling distribution becomes is important for us to know in determining if the normal distribution is a good fit for our sampling distribution. Knowing that the sampling distribution is normally or approximately normally distributed is important because we can standardize the sample mean with reference to the standard normal distribution using the following equation.

When the shape of the population distribution is normal or approximately normal and σ is known, then

$$z = \frac{\text{a value} - \text{its mean}}{\text{its standard deviation}} = \frac{\bar{x} - \mu_{\bar{x}}}{\sigma_{\bar{x}}} = \frac{\bar{x} - \mu}{\sigma / \sqrt{n}}$$

has a standard normal distribution. In other words, if the underlying population is itself normally distributed, then every distribution of sample means based on any sample size n will also be normally distributed.

When the Shape of the Distribution Is Unknown or Known to Be Not Normal

If the shape of the underlying population is either unknown or is known to be not normal, the sampling distribution of sample means may still be approximately normally distributed, but only when the sample size, n, is sufficiently large. If the sample size is sufficiently large, the sampling distribution of the mean is sufficiently concentrated around the mean that the sampling distribution is approximately normally distributed. Known as the Central Limit Theorem, the principle dynamic depends on the sample size, n.

The Central Limit Theorem states that the larger the sample size, n, the more nearly normally distributed is the sampling distribution of sample means based on random samples of n elements.

There are a number of qualifiers in our language here: "sufficiently," "approximately," "nearly." They play an important role in capturing the dynamic relationship between sample size, n, and the resulting shape of the sampling distribution of all sample means based on n elements. It is an important dynamic to understand because the sample size is most often a decision variable for the researcher to set. The sample size can be set at the beginning of data collection so that the resulting sample mean can be compared to a nearly normal distribution for analysis. How large does a sample size have to be so the researcher can be relatively confident the resulting sample mean can be compared to an approximately normal distribution? It can be shown mathematically that, for most populations, if the sample size is at least 30, the resulting sample mean can be compared to an approximately normal distribution.

When the shape of the population distribution is not normal but

- the population standard deviation, σ, is known and
- the sample size $n \geq 30$,

the sample mean can be compared to the standard normal distribution.

$$z = \frac{\text{a value} - \text{its mean}}{\text{its standard deviation}} = \frac{\bar{x} - \mu_{\bar{x}}}{\sigma_{\bar{x}}} = \frac{\bar{x} - \mu}{\sigma / \sqrt{n}}$$

In most applications of statistics, the population variance is not known. When the population variance is not known, two elements take on increased importance: the shape of the underlying population that was sampled and the size of the sample taken. As long as the underlying population is not heavily skewed and as long as the sample size is sufficiently large to satisfy requirements of the Central Limit Theorem, the t-distribution will be a good approximation of the sampling distribution, which uses the sample standard deviation, s, in place of the population standard deviation, σ.

When the shape of the population distribution is not normal and

- *s* from the sample is used in place of σ because σ is not known and
- the sample size $n \geq 30$,

the sample mean can be considered to be the *t*-distribution with $(n - 1)$ degrees of freedom.

$$t = \frac{\text{a value} - \text{its mean}}{\text{its standard deviation}} = \frac{\bar{x} - \mu_{\bar{x}}}{s_{\bar{x}}} = \frac{\bar{x} - \mu}{s/\sqrt{n}}$$

The larger the sample size *n* is, the better the approximation the *t*-distribution with $(n - 1)$ degrees of freedom is for the distribution of sample means. If the underlying population is not normal but is not heavily skewed, the *t*-distribution remains a reasonably good approximation of the sampling distribution of the mean as long as the sample size is sufficiently large to invoke the Central Limit Theorem.

Let's consider an example.

Example 3.4.

Suppose the average hourly production for a sample of 50 hours of assembly operations was 159.32 units with a standard deviation of 17.6. If the mean production level were actually 165 units per hour, how likely is it that we would get a sample of 50 hours with an average of 159.32 units or less?

Answer

The population hourly production level, or μ, is 165 units per hour. A sample of $n = 50$ hours of assembly operations represents $\bar{x} = 159.32$ with a sample standard deviation of $s = 17.6$ units per hour.

$$t = \frac{\bar{x} - \mu}{s/\sqrt{n}} = \frac{159.32 - 165}{17.6/\sqrt{50}} = -2.282$$

$$P(\bar{x} < 159.32) = P(t < -2.282)$$

The t-coefficient falls between $t_{.01} = -2.407$ and $t_{.025} = -2.010$. From the t-table, all we can say is that the probability falls between 0.01 and 0.025. Using Excel, we can use the TDIST function to determine the exact value of the probability at 0.013434.

Interpretation: There is a 1.34% chance that a sample of 50 hours will produce an average hourly production of 159.32 units or less when the true population mean production is 165 units per hour. While it is possible that the average hourly production level of 159.32 units or less can occur when the real population production level is 165 units per hour, it is not very likely to occur.

Understanding the Behavior of Sample Proportions

Measurements generate continuous quantitative data that are typically summarized with means and standard deviations. Counts are discrete data typically summarized with proportions. Theoretically, the appropriate distribution for discrete data is a member of the set of discrete distributions. Discrete distributions are complex to work with computationally, however, and it has been shown that if the sample sizes are sufficiently large, the z-distribution is a very good approximation of the sampling distribution of the proportion that is created by a ratio of the counts generated.

Proportion

$$\text{For a population: } p = \frac{x}{N}$$

$$\text{For a sample: } \bar{p} = \frac{x}{n}$$

where

x = the number of elements satisfying the condition of interest,

N = the size of the population, and

n = the size of the sample.

To reasonably estimate a discrete distribution with the z-distribution, the sample size must be large enough for the product of $n \cdot p$ and $n \cdot (1 - p)$ to be greater than or equal to 5. Realistically, only the smaller of the values p and $(1 - p)$ must be tested. The closer the population proportion is to 0.5, the smaller the required sample size is to meet the conditions stated above. For example, if $p = 0.5$, a sample size of 10 would be sufficient. If $p = 0.1$, however, a sample size of at least 50 is required. If $p = 0.8$, a sample size of at least 25 would be required, since $(1 - 0.8) = 0.2$ and $0.2 \times 25 = 5$.

When both $n \cdot p \geq 5$ and $n \cdot (1 - p) \geq 5$,

$$z = \frac{\bar{p} - p}{\sigma_{\bar{p}}} = \frac{\bar{p} - p}{\sqrt{\dfrac{p \cdot (1 - p)}{n}}}$$

has approximately a standard normal distribution, where $\bar{p}$ is the sample proportion, p is the population proportion, and n is the sample size.

Let's consider an example.

Example 3.5.

According to the Food Marketing Institute, approximately 22% of all grocery shoppers do most of their shopping on Saturday. How likely is it that a random sample of 72 shoppers indicates that fewer than 12% do their grocery shopping on Saturday?

Answer

The sample proportion is 12%, the population proportion is 22%, and the sample size is 72.

$$z = \frac{\bar{p} - p}{\sqrt{\dfrac{p \cdot (1 - p)}{n}}} = \frac{0.12 - 0.22}{\sqrt{\dfrac{0.22 \cdot (1 - 0.22)}{72}}} = -2.048 \approx -2.05$$

$$P(\bar{p} < 0.12) = P(z < -2.05) = 0.02$$

Interpretation: There is a 2% chance that a sample of 72 homes will produce a sample proportion of 12% or less who do most of their grocery shopping on Saturday. While it is possible that the proportion of shoppers will have 12% or less who do most of their grocery shopping on Saturdays, it is not very likely to occur.

Point and Interval Estimates

Sometimes what we need is a good estimate of the value for an important variable. How much income do we anticipate generating during the next fiscal year? What proportion of a region's population served by the community's hospital will require emergency room treatment during the next month? A point estimate is the single value that best approximates the value of a population parameter of interest. If we take a random sample from a population and compute the sample mean, $\bar{x}$, this would serve as a point estimate of the true population mean, μ. If we want to estimate the proportion of a population that falls in a particular category, the sample proportion, $\bar{p}$, would serve as the point estimate of the true population proportion, p.

In contrast, an interval estimate is a set of numbers centered at the point estimate and extending above and below the point estimate. Because of sampling error, we know a sample statistic will not be exactly equal to the parameter it estimates. An interval estimate allows for the occurrence of sampling error. More exactly, an interval estimate is constructed from n sample data in a way that a specified percent of all possible samples of size n taken from the same population will contain the true value of the population parameter.

Under certain assumptions, using a z- or t-coefficient allows us to accommodate and control for the sampling error in our estimates of the population mean or proportion. Earlier in this chapter, we calculated the z- or the t-value based on data from the sample to determine the probability that the sample statistic would fall in a certain range. Here, our use of a particular z- or t-coefficient is to determine a likely range for our estimate of the population mean or proportion. The coefficient is derived from the appropriate table based on the amount of confidence we want to have that our interval will contain the true population mean or proportion. The amount of risk we are willing to sustain is $100(\alpha)\%$, and the amount of confidence we want to have is $100(1 - \alpha)\%$, where α is pronounced *alpha*. We will expand our discussion and use of alpha in Chapter 4.

Confidence Intervals on the Mean

Algebraically we can derive the equation for the confidence interval for a mean from the equation we used earlier to standardize means. We begin with the definition of the *z*-coefficient, $\pm z = \dfrac{\bar{x} - \mu}{\sigma / \sqrt{n}}$. We then multiply both sides of the equation by the denominator of the right-hand side, $\sigma / \sqrt{n}$, which is the standard error of the mean,

$$\pm z \cdot \sigma / \sqrt{n} = \frac{\bar{x} - \mu}{\sigma / \sqrt{n}} \cdot \sigma / \sqrt{n}$$

arriving at the equation for the *z*-confidence interval, $\bar{x} \pm z \cdot \dfrac{\sigma}{\sqrt{n}}$. The equation for a *t*-confidence interval can be derived in the same way, giving us the equation for the *t*-confidence interval, $\bar{x} \pm t \cdot \dfrac{s}{\sqrt{n}}$.

Geometrically, the structure of the interval is perhaps more easily understood. The product of the *z*- or *t*-coefficient times the standard error of the mean is actually the distance between the center of the interval, in this case $\bar{x}$, and either the upper or the lower interval bound. Two times that product is the width of the entire interval, so the product of the *z*- or *t*-coefficient times the standard error of the mean is called the *interval half-width*. The lower bound of the confidence interval is the point estimate minus the interval half-width and the upper bound of the confidence interval is the point estimate plus the interval half-width.

We can construct an interval that functions in essence as a measuring tape, so that, between its lower and upper bounds, the population

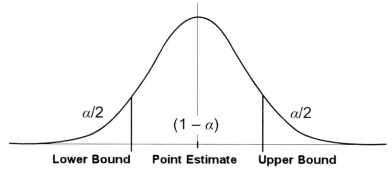

Figure 3.1. The 100(1 − α)% Confidence Interval

parameter will fall in a stated percent of all possible sample intervals of size *n* taken from that population. If we want to be $100(1 - \alpha)\%$ confident that samples of a certain width will contain the population parameter, then we select the *z*- or *t*-coefficient associated with that level of confidence. Alternatively, we can conclude that, over a large number of repeated samples of the same sample size *n*, $100(1 - \alpha)\%$ of the sample means will fall between the lower and the upper confidence interval bounds.

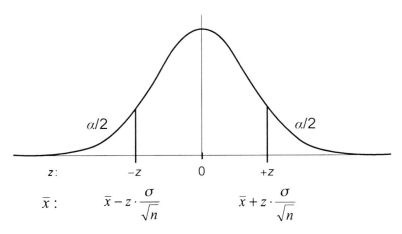

Figure 3.2. The *z*-Confidence Interval on $\bar{x}$

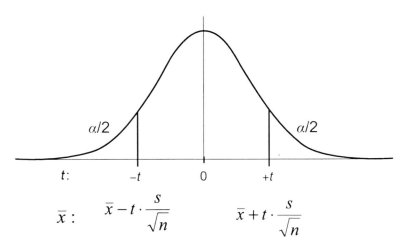

Figure 3.3. The *t*-Confidence Interval on $\bar{x}$

For z-confidence intervals, the population standard deviation, σ, must be known and either the underlying population being sampled is approximately normally distributed, or the sample size n must be sufficiently large to invoke the Central Limit Theorem. For t-confidence intervals, the population standard deviation, σ, is not known, so we use the sample standard deviation, s, in its place. Additionally, the underlying population being sampled must be normally distributed. In both confidence intervals, the samples must be randomly chosen for any inference to hold about the population being sampled.

Example 3.6.

A food processing company makes tortilla chips. Although its 16-ounce bags of chips are routinely sampled for compliance with the stated product weight, the company has recently renewed sampling individual bags for the number of chips each contained. Historic data indicate the number of chips per bag is normally distributed with a standard deviation of 38. A random sample of 50 16-ounce bags taken from yesterday's production run yielded a sample mean of 176.4 chips per bag. Between what two bounds on the number of tortilla chips per 16-ounce bag can we be 95% confident that the interval contains the true process mean?

Answer

Because the population standard deviation is given ($\sigma = 38$) and the population is known to be normally distributed, we will use a z-confidence interval to establish bounds on the mean number of chips per 16-ounce bag. To be 95% confident, the 5% risk we are wrong is split between the upper and lower tails of the distribution. The appropriate z-coefficient is $z = \pm1.96$. The sample size is given, $n = 50$, and the sample mean is given, $\bar{x} = 176.4$.

$$\text{Upper bound: } \bar{x} + z \cdot \frac{\sigma}{\sqrt{n}} = 176.4 + 1.96 \cdot \frac{38}{\sqrt{50}} = 176.4 + 10.53 = 186.93$$

$$\text{Lower bound: } \bar{x} - z \cdot \frac{\sigma}{\sqrt{n}} = 176.4 - 1.96 \cdot \frac{38}{\sqrt{50}} = 176.4 - 10.53 = 165.87$$

Interpretation: We can be 95% confident that if we tested all bags of tortilla chips, the true mean number of chips per bag will fall between 165.87 and 186.93.

Confidence Intervals on the Proportion

Algebraically we can derive the equation for the confidence interval for a proportion much as we did for the confidence interval on a mean, with one significant difference. We are working with sample data only, so the standard error of the proportion, $\sigma_{\bar{p}}$, is formed on the sample proportion:

$\sigma_{\bar{p}} = \sqrt{\dfrac{\bar{p} \cdot (1 - \bar{p})}{n}}$, which leads us to the equation for the z-confidence interval, $\bar{p} \pm z \cdot \sqrt{\dfrac{\bar{p} \cdot (1 - \bar{p})}{n}}$.

Example 3.7.

A manufacturer of drip irrigation controllers is interested in reporting an interval estimate for the proportion of manufactured units that are defective. A random sample of 800 controllers determined that 12 were defective. Between what two bounds can we be 90% confident that the interval estimate contains the true defective rate for all drip irrigation controllers?

Answer

Since the number of defective controllers (12) and the number of fully functional controllers (788) are both greater than 5, we will use a z-confidence interval to establish bounds on the defective rate. To be 90% confident, the 10% risk we are wrong is split between the upper and lower tails of the distribution. The appropriate z-coefficient is $z = \pm 1.645$. The sample proportion is found by dividing the number of defective controllers by the overall sample size, $\bar{p} = \dfrac{12}{800} = 0.015$.

Upper bound: $\bar{p} + z \cdot \sqrt{\dfrac{\bar{p} \cdot (1 - \bar{p})}{n}} = 0.015 + 1.645 \cdot \sqrt{\dfrac{0.015 \cdot 0.985}{800}}$

$$= 0.015 + 0.007 = 0.022$$

$$\text{Lower bound: } \overline{p} - z \cdot \sqrt{\frac{\overline{p} \cdot (1 - \overline{p})}{n}} = 0.015 - 1.645 \cdot \sqrt{\frac{0.015 \cdot 0.985}{800}}$$

$$= 0.015 - 0.007 = 0.008$$

Interpretation: We can be 90% confident that if we tested all irrigation controllers, the defective rate will fall between 0.8% and 2.2%.

CHAPTER 4

Using Proof by Contradiction to Draw Conclusions

Uncertainty is a fact of life. We often have good evidence to support our claims or our beliefs. We seldom have irrefutable evidence of the important ones. In statistics, the process by which we gather information and link it as evidence to our claims or beliefs is called scientific, or hypothesis, testing. It is, at its heart, a proof by contradiction. A proof by contradiction goes something like this:

1. Assume as true the opposite of what you are testing for.
2. Envision what data should look like if that opposite were, in fact, true.
3. Gather data relating to the claims, and compare the vision for the data and the actual data gathered.
4. Draw a conclusion from the comparison and interpret its meaning in terms of the research question.

What researchers hope to draw is a negative conclusion. That is, researchers want to show that the data they gathered are so unlikely to come from a world in which the assumption made in step 1 is true that they must conclude the assumption is not true, is contradicted. Some new terminology will help us develop this chain of logic. The null hypothesis is a formal statement about the population that is consistent with the assumption in step 1. Often the null hypothesis is a statement about a population parameter that characterizes what has been typical of the population in the past, that nothing will change in that population, that the *status quo* will continue. It is denoted by H_0. The alternative hypothesis is the challenge posed by research that, if shown true, will cause a change to the *status quo*. It is sometimes called the research hypothesis since it is the reason the research is undertaken in the first place. It is denoted by H_1 and is stated in a manner that is the opposite of the statement in the null hypothesis, H_0.

The Hypotheses: Making a Claim

Forming hypotheses is the first step of any analytic project. Because it contains the reason for the research, the alternative hypothesis is often easier to form first. Let's investigate several research scenarios.

Scenario 1: Product containers are filled with 6 ounces (170 grams) of salted nuts. If the containers are overfilled, the product does not ship well and does not hold its shelf life. If the containers are underfilled, the company risks a fine from consumer advocates. Samples of 50 containers are randomly selected and individual product weights are taken and recorded. If the containers are either over or under filled, the quality control officer will halt the production line and schedule maintenance to service the machines.

In Scenario 1, the quality control officer will continue production as usual as long as the average container weight is 6 ounces. The officer will alter the current production flow if there is evidence that the average container weight is not 6 ounces. So the best null and alternative hypotheses are the following:

$$H_0: \mu = 6 \qquad\qquad H_1: \mu \neq 6$$

This is a nondirectional, two-tailed test.

Scenario 2: The air quality index (AQI) is a system used by local and national agencies to report on how clean or polluted the air is. The AQI ranges from 0, which indicates no risk of pollution, to 500, which carries a hazardous warning for the entire population. An AQI in the range of 101 to 150 means the air is unhealthy for sensitive groups, who may experience some health effects as a result of air pollution. If the AQI is 150 or less, the general public is not likely to be affected. If the AQI is above 150, everyone may begin to experience health effects. If the AQI is above 150, a media announcement is activated to warn local residents that air quality is unhealthy.

In Scenario 2, the general public is not at risk if the AQI is 150 or less. The general public is at risk if the AQI is above 150. To determine whether the air quality is good and the general public is at little or no health risk as a result, or whether air quality is sufficiently bad to cause some health risk to the general public, the best null and alternative hypotheses are the following:

$$H_0: \mu \leq 150 \qquad\qquad H_1: \mu > 150$$

This is a directional, upper-tailed test.

Scenario 3: Regional management for a large chain of home construction and improvement stores has indicated that at least 60% of all items on their store shelves must have individual prices marked on the items. Individual store managers are being notified that inspectors will be surveying shelved inventories. Managers of stores that do not meet the guideline will be cited.

In Scenario 3, managers will not be cited if 60% or more of their shelved inventories are marked with the item price. Managers will be cited if less than 60% of their shelved inventories are marked with the item price. So the best null and alternative hypotheses are the following:

$$H_0: p \geq 0.60 \qquad\qquad H_1: p < 0.60$$

This is a directional, lower-tailed test.

In all three scenarios, *the entire number line is covered by the null and alternative hypotheses*. This is true, in fact, of all pairs of null and alternative hypotheses. This is also true whether the hypothesis test is two-tailed, as in Scenario 1, or one-tailed, as in Scenarios 2 and 3. A second important point arises from investigating these three scenarios: in all three scenarios, *the equal sign is included in the null hypothesis*. This too is true of all pairs of null and alternative hypotheses. It means that there must be more than enough evidence to conclude the alternative hypothesis is true to warrant changing the *status quo*.

A final but important note about forming hypotheses: while the contexts given in this book are predefined as appropriate for a one- or two-tailed test, the researcher should be careful about structuring a one-tailed hypothesis test. Two-tailed tests are generally most appropriate except where reason, historic record, or known effects persuade the researcher to structure and perform a one-tailed test.

The Decision Rule: Setting Error Tolerance

With hypotheses in place, the researcher next must play out the null hypothesis. The null hypothesis is assumed to be true. The researcher must ask: if the null hypothesis were true, what should we expect to see? In the formal hypothesis test, this step creates a decision rule. For example, if, in Scenario 1, the mean is equal to 6 ounces, then sample means will likely fall no further than some specified number of units of standard error away from the center, 6 ounces. If, in Scenario 2, the mean AQI is less than or equal to 150, then air samples will generate means that are no more than a specific number of units of standard error above 150. If, in Scenario 3, the proportion is greater than or equal to 0.60, then sample proportions taken from that population will fall no less than some specified number of units of standard error below 0.60.

While a well-adjusted production line may occasionally produce a sample of 50 containers whose average weight is well above or below the intended mean of 6 ounces, it is not very probable to occur. After all, when the machines truly are well adjusted, that means they are achieving an average fill of 6 ounces per container. In evaluating a sample mean that occurs outside the expected window of production on either side of the mean of 6 ounces, making a decision to stop the line and schedule maintenance to adjust the machines requires the quality control manager to accept a certain level of risk that the decision is in error. That risk is called a Type I error and is denoted by α. Alpha (α) is the probability that a true null hypothesis is incorrectly rejected. In the research scenario, the sample mean is all the decision maker has, however, to then infer whether the sample could have come from a population located at μ. A decision maker cannot be 100% certain that the sample whose mean falls in an outer tail isn't just an odd sample that really did come from a sampling distribution whose mean is located at μ. So the decision maker must accept a Type I error of probability α in order to set a limit on how unusual a sample can be before they decide that the sample is just too different to believe it came from a population that was actually centered at μ. The critical bound defines that limit. Since $100\alpha\%$ is the error a researcher is willing to accept, $100(1 - \alpha)\%$ is the level of confidence the decision maker has in deciding the hypothesis test results.

In a one-tailed hypothesis test, α appears in one tail of the distribution. In fact, α appears in the tail that the alternative hypothesis designates. The Type I error, α, is the amount of area left in the tail beyond the critical z or t bound, or the amount of area in the rejection region, as shown in Figures 4.1 and 4.2.

In a two-tailed hypothesis test, the Type I error, α, is split between the upper and lower tail. So the amount of area in any one tail of the distribution is $\alpha/2$, as shown in Figure 4.3. The amount of error in deciding the hypothesis test is still α, and the amount of confidence the researcher has in the results continues to be $100(1 - \alpha)\%$.

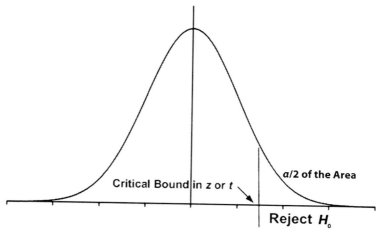

Figure 4.1. An Upper-Tailed Test

H_0: A population parameter $\leq$ A specific value
H_1: A population parameter $>$ A specific value

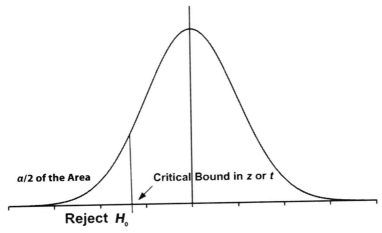

Figure 4.2. A Lower-Tailed Test

H_0: A population parameter $\geq$ A specific value

H_1: A population parameter $<$ A specific value

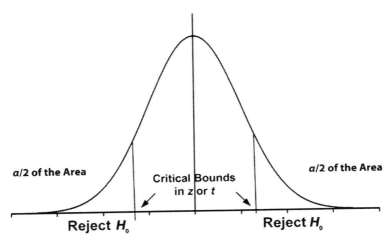

Figure 4.3. Two-Tailed Test

H_0: A population parameter $=$ A specific value

H_1: A population parameter $\neq$ A specific value

The Test Statistic

Evaluating the sample data is perhaps the easiest step of conducting a hypothesis test. At this stage, the researcher should collect the data and calculate the sample statistics (for example, $\bar{x}$, s, or $\bar{p}$). Using the values of the sample statistics and hypothesized value of the population parameter, the test statistic (for example, z or t) can be calculated.

Compared to the first step of framing appropriate null and alternative hypotheses, and the second step of determining an appropriate Type I error and decision rule, the third step of computing the sample statistic is relatively straightforward. Gathering good data may be time consuming, but the design for gathering and analyzing the data should be completed in the first two steps of the research project. As we will see later in this chapter, we will use one of several general equations in computing a statistic that we will then compare to the acceptable window around the population measure.

Good research practice should complete the statement of hypotheses and the decision rule *before* collecting the data and calculating the statistics. Even if the data were technically collected in advance of the study, prior analysis of the data should not be used to structure the hypotheses or set the error tolerance.

Drawing a Conclusion

The fourth step in the process of hypothesis testing is drawing a conclusion and tying it specifically to the problem environment. The sense of the conclusion we draw is not a statement of immutable truth, nor is it something we can say with absolute certainty. The conclusion is a statement based on probability. It is probably true. There is a small chance that the decision is in error. Reaching a conclusion is perhaps best characterized as an assertion warranted by the evidence we have brought to bear on the null hypothesis. As such, when we state the conclusion, we should reflect the sample statistic, the decision rule, the conclusion, and the amount of confidence we have in making the statement. A second statement is useful in reflecting back on the problem environment to indicate what the conclusion means in the problem's context.

In summary, then, a formal hypothesis test should include the following:

1. The null hypothesis and the alternative hypothesis
2. The decision rule, which includes both a statement of the Type I error the decision maker is willing to accept in order to make a decision, as well as the acceptable window around the population measure
3. The value of the sample statistic
4. The conclusion and its interpretation

One final note about hypothesis testing: a proof by contradiction requires that the null hypothesis is assumed to be true. The conclusion can refute that assumption, or not. That is, the researcher can conclude that the test statistic is so unusual, the sample cannot have come from a population centered at μ. Or the researcher can conclude that the test statistic is not unusual enough to reject the null hypothesis. What the researcher cannot conclude is that the null hypothesis must be true. Why not? Because the null hypothesis was assumed to be true to begin with, a researcher cannot then conclude that the null hypothesis must be true. That would constitute circular logic: you cannot prove true what you assumed was true in the first place. To avoid this fundamental error in logic, we adopt the convention of concluding either that we have sufficient evidence to reject the null hypothesis or we do not have sufficient evidence to allow us to reject the null hypothesis. We cannot conclude that we accept the null hypothesis.

The p-Value: The Observed Significance Level

The observed significance level, known as the p-value, is based on two elements of the hypothesis test: the value of the test statistic and the hypotheses being tested. While the level of significance of the test, α, is a value the decision maker sets at the beginning of the research, the observed significance level, the p-value, is determined by the results of the sample data. The p-value is the probability that a sample statistic based on another random sample selected from the same population is at least as extreme as the calculated sample statistic. Because it is based on the sample statistic, the p-value is called the observed significance level of the test statistic.

The p-value is a measure of how different the sample is from the hypothesized population. A p-value can be calculated for any sample statistic as it relates to its theoretical distribution. We will discuss p-values for test statistics related to the t-distribution, the z-distribution, the F-distribution, and the χ^2-distribution. The p-value is particularly useful because it cuts across theoretical distributions. It is often referenced in publications following a research conclusion, shown in parentheses to communicate the strength of the evidence supporting the research conclusion.

In a one-tailed hypothesis test, the p-value is the amount of area beyond the test statistic into the tail of the rejection region. To find it on the z-distribution, we simply look the test statistic up on the Cumulative Standard Normal Table. If the p-value is smaller than α, then the test statistic itself falls beyond the critical bound of the rejection region. When that happens, the null hypothesis is rejected. If the p-value is larger than α, then the test statistic falls between the population parameter and the boundary of the rejection region. When that happens, the null hypothesis cannot be rejected.

In a two-tailed hypothesis test, sample data are just as likely to be positive as negative. So the amount of area beyond the test statistic into the tail of the distribution is only half of the p-value. To get the full p-value, the area beyond the test statistic has to be doubled. Comparisons of the p-value and α are then conducted as indicated in a one-tailed hypothesis test.

Testing Hypotheses Involving μ When σ Is Known

Human behavior and performance typically vary widely and vary differently over different populations. When dealing with human performance, it is usually the case that variance on their measures is not known. Some exceptions occur when significant historical data exist from which accurate evaluations of variance can be derived. In contrast, many mechanical processes are designed so that mean performance and variance on mean performance can be controlled within machine tolerances.

In instances where σ is known and the underlying population is normally distributed, the sampling distribution of the mean will be normally distributed regardless of the sample size taken. In instances where σ is known but the underlying population is not normally distributed, sampling distributions of the mean are approximately normally distributed when the sample size is sufficiently large. Knowing that the sampling distribution of the mean is normally or approximately normally distributed allows us to standardize the sample mean with reference to the standard normal distribution using the following equation:

---

z-Test for H_0: μ {=, ≥, ≤} a Specific Value When σ Is Known

The Test Statistic:

$$z = \frac{\text{a sample mean} - \text{the hypothesized value}}{\text{the standard error}} = \frac{\bar{x} - \mu}{\sigma / \sqrt{n}}$$

where the hypothesized value for μ is specified in the null hypothesis, H_0.

Example 4.1.

A commercial processing plant fills containers with 6 ounces (170 grams) of salted nuts. Machinery on the production line is set to maintain a variance of 0.008 ounces. If the containers are either over or under filled, the quality control officer will halt the production line and schedule maintenance to service the machines. Samples of 50 containers are randomly selected and individual product weights are taken and recorded. The last sample of 50 containers produced a mean of 5.9775 ounces. Should the line be shut down for maintenance? Use a 5% level of significance.

Answer

H_0: $\mu = 6$ H_1: $\mu \neq 6$

Average container weight is 6 ounces. The machinery does not need additional service.

Average container weight is not 6 ounces. The machinery does need additional service.

Decision Rule: Since this is a two-tailed test, the alpha level of 0.05 is split in half, half allocated to the upper tail and half to the lower tail of the rejection region. See Figure 4.3. For $\alpha = 0.05$, then, we identify the critical bound associated with an 0.9750 on the z-table, because the central area of 0.95 and the lower tail of 0.025 are combined. We will reject the null hypothesis if the calculated test statistic falls above $z = 1.96$ or below $z = -1.96$.

Test Statistic:

$$\sigma^2 = 0.008 \qquad \sigma = \sqrt{0.008} = 0.0894$$

$$z = \frac{\bar{x} - \mu}{\sigma / \sqrt{n}} = \frac{5.9775 - 6}{0.0894 / \sqrt{50}} = -1.78$$

Observed Significance Level: For a z-score of -1.78, the probability is 0.0375 of getting a z-score of -1.78 or more negative. Since this is a two-tailed test, the test statistic could just as likely be $+1.78$ or greater. So the area below the z of -1.78 is only half of the total area to be included. The full p-value is then twice the area captured below the test statistic of $z = -1.78$.

$$p\text{-value} = 2 \cdot (0.0375) = 0.0750$$

Conclusion: Since the test statistic of $z = -1.78$ falls between the critical bounds of ± 1.96, we do not reject H_0 with at least 95% confidence. Likewise, since the p-value of 0.0750 is greater than the desired α of 0.05, we do not reject H_0. There is not enough evidence to conclude the machinery needs additional service. The line should not be shut down for maintenance.

Connection Between the Hypothesis Test and the Confidence Interval

In Chapter 3, we introduced the notion and calculations for the confidence interval. We looked at confidence intervals on the mean and on the proportion. Although the goal of a confidence interval is different from the goal of a hypothesis test, there is still a very real connection between them. Put simply, for the two-tailed hypothesis test, if the value we test in the null hypothesis falls between the upper and lower bounds of the confidence interval, the conclusion of the hypothesis test will not reject H_0. And, for the two-tailed hypothesis test, if the value we test in the null hypothesis falls outside of the confidence interval bounds, the conclusion of the hypothesis test will reject H_0. For a one-tailed hypothesis test, we should compare the value in the null hypothesis to the confidence interval bounds calculated for twice the value of the significance level used for the hypothesis test, so that $100\alpha\%$ of the area is in both the rejection region of the hypothesis test and one tail of the confidence interval. To demonstrate the connection, we return to Example 4.1 and compute the 95% confidence interval around the sample mean of 5.9775:

$$\bar{x} \pm z \cdot \frac{\sigma}{\sqrt{n}} = 5.9775 \pm 1.96 \cdot \frac{0.0894}{\sqrt{50}} = 5.9775 \pm 0.0248$$

The lower bound on the mean container weight is 5.9527 ounces, and the upper bound is 6.0023 ounces. Since the hypothesized mean of 6 ounces is contained in the 95% confidence interval around the sample mean, we fail to reject the comparable hypothesis that the true mean could be different from 6 ounces based on this sample with the comparable 95% confidence level.

Testing Hypotheses Involving μ When σ Is Unknown

When the population variance, σ, is not known, the sample size must be sufficiently large to satisfy requirements of the Central Limit Theorem for us to use the t-distribution as an approximation of the sampling distribution.

---

t-Test for H_0: μ {=, ≥, ≤} a Specific Value When σ Is Unknown

The Test Statistic:

$$t = \frac{\text{a sample mean} - \text{the hypothesized value}}{\text{the standard error}} = \frac{\bar{x} - \mu}{s / \sqrt{n}}$$

where the hypothesized value for μ is specified in the null hypothesis, H_0.

We need to discuss the process of identifying the appropriate t-coefficient to use as the critical bound in hypothesis tests using the t as the test statistic. To identify the critical bound in t, we enter the t-table with two pieces of information from the problem we wish to solve: (1) the degrees of freedom, and (2) the amount of area in the tail of the t-distribution. In the case of an upper-tail t-test with, for example, 7 degrees of freedom and $\alpha = 0.05$, we would identify $t = 1.895$ as the appropriate critical bound for the rejection region. In the case of a lower-tail t-test with 7 degrees of freedom and $\alpha = 0.05$, we would identify $t = -1.895$ as the appropriate critical bound for the rejection region.

Table 4.1. *Finding the Critical Bound in t for df = 7 and 0.05 in the Tail*

The Student's t-Distribution					
α =	**0.10**	**0.05**	**0.025**	**0.01**	**0.005**
df = 1	3.078	6.314	12.706	31.821	63.656
2	1.886	2.920	4.303	6.965	9.925
3	1.638	2.353	3.182	4.541	5.841
4	1.533	2.132	2.776	3.747	4.604
5	1.476	2.015	2.571	3.365	4.032
6	1.440	1.943	2.447	3.143	3.707
7	1.415	1.895	2.365	2.998	3.499
8	1.397	1.860	2.306	2.896	3.355

In the case of a two-tailed *t*-test with 7 degrees of freedom and α = 0.05, we would identify t = ±2.365 as the appropriate critical bounds for the rejection region.

Table 4.2. *Finding the Critical Bound in t for df = 7 and 0.025 in the Tail*

The Student's t-Distribution					
α =	**0.10**	**0.05**	**0.025**	**0.01**	**0.005**
df = 1	3.078	6.314	12.706	31.821	63.656
2	1.886	2.920	4.303	6.965	9.925
3	1.638	2.353	3.182	4.541	5.841
4	1.533	2.132	2.776	3.747	4.604
5	1.476	2.015	2.571	3.365	4.032
6	1.440	1.943	2.447	3.143	3.707
7	1.415	1.895	2.365	2.998	3.499
8	1.397	1.860	2.306	2.896	3.355

Example 4.2.

According to the Food Marketing Institute, the average sales per customer transaction for supermarkets in the United States was $27.61 in 2008. Suppose management of a regionally owned supermarket believed their average sales per customer transaction is higher than the value for the nation as a whole. They took a random sample of 60 customer transactions and found their mean to be $31.24 with a standard deviation of $8.15. Is there sufficient evidence to conclude with 99% confidence that their average customer transaction is higher than the average for the nation as a whole?

Answer

$H_0: \mu \le \$27.61$ $H_1: \mu > \$27.61$

Average sales per customer   Average sales per customer
transaction is less than or equal   transaction is greater than
to $27.61. $27.61.

Because the population value σ is not known, we use the sample value s to approximate it. So we use the t-distribution, not the z-distribution.

Decision Rule: Since this is a one-tailed test, the alpha level of 0.01 is entirely in the upper tail of the rejection region. See Figure 4.1. For $\alpha = 0.01$ with 59 degrees of freedom, we will reject the null hypothesis if the calculated test statistic falls above $t = 2.391$.

Test Statistic:

$$t = \frac{\bar{x} - \mu}{s/\sqrt{n}} = \frac{\$31.24 - \$27.61}{\$8.15/\sqrt{60}} = 3.45$$

Observed Significance Level: To find an exact p-value for a t statistic, we use Excel's imbedded function $=tdist(3.45,59,1)$, which yields the answer: p-value $= 0.000521$.

Conclusion: Since the test statistic of $t = 3.45$ falls above the critical bound of 2.391, we reject H_0 with at least 99% confidence. Likewise, since the p-value of 0.0005 is less than the desired α of 0.01, we reject H_0. There is enough evidence to conclude that the average sales per customer transaction for this regionally owned supermarket is higher than the average for the nation as a whole.

Testing Hypotheses Involving p When n Is Sufficiently Large

- Who does the grocery shopping more often for a typical household? The male or the female head of household?
- What proportion of vehicles involved in traffic crashes are light trucks?

- What percent of plumbing parts shipped to retailers and distributors last year were domestically made?
- Is your favorite candidate leading by a comfortable margin two weeks before the election?
- Does the percent of defective products produced increase during the night shifts?

Sometimes what we want to know cannot be measured. In answering the sample of questions above, we would not measure things but count them. We would count male and female heads of households who report more often doing the grocery shopping; the total number of traffic crashes and the number that involved light trucks; the total number of plumbing parts made last year and the number that were domestically made, etc. Theoretically, the appropriate distribution to reference is a discrete distribution because the underlying variables are discrete counts. It has been shown that if the sample sizes are sufficiently large, the z-distribution is a very good approximation of the sampling distribution of the proportion that is created by a ratio of the counts generated. To successfully convert a discrete distribution to the z-distribution, both $n \cdot p$ and $n \cdot (1 - p)$ must be greater than or equal to 5.

---

z-Test for H_0: p {=, ≥, ≤} a Specific Value

The Test Statistic:

$$z = \frac{\text{sample proportion - population proportion}}{\text{standard error of the proportion}} = \frac{\bar{p} - p}{\sqrt{\dfrac{p \cdot (1 - p)}{n}}}$$

where the value of the population proportion, p, is specified in the hull hypothesis, H_0.

Example 4.3.

According to the American Institute of Architects in their second quarter 2010 survey, 31.3% of residential architects identified an in-home office as the most popular special feature of new households. Suppose a random sample of 100 homebuilders reported that 28% of new homebuyers were specifically looking for a residence with an in-home office. Are homebuilders reporting results that differ significantly from the information provided by the American Institute of Architects? Use a 90% level of confidence.

Answer

$H_0: p = 0.313$ $H_1: p \neq 0.313$

The proportion of homebuyers who are specifically looking for a residence with an in-home office is the same as the information provided by the American Institute of Architects.

The proportion of homebuyers who are specifically looking for a residence with an in-home office differs from the information provided by the American Institute of Architects.

Decision Rule: For $\alpha = 0.10$, we will reject the null hypothesis if the calculated test statistic falls above $z = 1.645$ or below $z = -1.645$.

Test Statistic:

$$z = \frac{\bar{p} - p}{\sqrt{\dfrac{p \cdot (1-p)}{n}}} = \frac{0.28 - 0.313}{\sqrt{\dfrac{0.313 \cdot (1 - 0.313)}{100}}} = -0.71$$

Observed Significance Level: p-value $= 2 \cdot (0.2389) = 0.4778$

Conclusion: Since the test statistic of $z = -0.71$ falls between the critical bounds of ± 1.645, we do not reject H_0 with at least 90% confidence. Likewise, since the p-value of 0.4778 is greater than the desired α of 0.10, we do not reject H_0. There is not enough evidence to conclude that the proportion of homebuyers differ significantly from the information provided by the American Institute of Architects (http://www.aia.org/practicing/AIAB085952).

CHAPTER 5

Testing Two Population Means and Proportions

The ability to compare two population parameters is both useful and important in expanding the roles estimation and hypothesis testing can play in analyzing sample data. In this chapter, we continue our discussion of population means, variances, and proportions, but we develop the analysis to compare differences between two population means and differences between two proportions. The underlying logic of hypothesis testing remains unchanged.

We encounter several complexities in expanding our analysis to two populations that we did not find in dealing with a single population. In analyzing differences between population means, we separate those that are estimated with independent samples taken from two unrelated populations and those that are estimated with dependent samples taken from two closely related populations. Samples taken from two populations are independent when a random sample of elements is drawn from each population separately. If, on the other hand, we construct samples so that each element in the sample from one population corresponds to, or is paired with, an element in the sample from the second population, we have dependent samples. We continue to work with the z- and the t- distributions but find there are two different t-tests to use depending on whether the population variances are equal or unequal.

The t-Test for Differences Between Two Means Given Independent Samples and Equal Variances

We introduce the t-test first because it is so frequently used. More often than not, we deal with samples taken from populations for which we do not know their population standard deviation, σ. The t-test is considered a robust test even if the underlying populations are not normal because it still generates reasonably accurate results if the sample sizes are large enough to invoke the Central Limit Theorem.

Inferences about the difference between population means $(\mu_1 - \mu_2)$ taken from two independent samples are based on two random samples from two unrelated populations. The two samples do not have to be the same size, and nothing about the way in which one sample is selected from the first population affects the elements that are sampled from the second population. Because we are estimating two population parameters, the degrees of freedom for use with the t-distribution are combined from each of the samples: $df = (n_1 - 1) + (n_2 - 1)$, or $df = (n_1 + n_2 - 2)$.

Later in this chapter, we will discuss a statistical test to settle the question of whether two population variances are different enough that we should consider them unequal. For this text section, we will assume the population variances are roughly equal. So, given we assume the two variances are equal, we act accordingly. We combine the two sample variances and form a single pooled variance estimate, s_p^2, which is the two sample variances weighted, or multiplied, by their individual degrees of freedom and averaged across their combined degrees of freedom.

The Pooled Variance Estimate, s_p^2

$$s_p^2 = \frac{(n_1 - 1) \cdot s_1^2 + (n_2 - 1) \cdot s_2^2}{n_1 + n_2 - 2}$$

where n_1 and n_2 are the sample sizes and s_1^2 and s_2^2 are the variances from the two samples.

The test statistic is determined by the same general equation we have seen in previous chapters

---

t-Test of Two Means Assuming Equal Variances

$$t = \frac{\text{the sample statistic} - \text{hypothesized difference contained in } H_0}{\text{the standard error of the sample statistic}}$$

$$= \frac{(\bar{x}_1 - \bar{x}_2) - (\mu_1 - \mu_2)}{s_{(\bar{x}_1 - \bar{x}_2)}} = \frac{(\bar{x}_1 - \bar{x}_2) - (\mu_1 - \mu_2)}{\sqrt{s_p^2 \cdot \left(\dfrac{1}{n_1} + \dfrac{1}{n_2}\right)}}$$

where n_1 and n_2 are the sample sizes, s_p^2 is the pooled variance estimate from the two samples, and $(\mu - \mu_2)$ is the value shown in H_0.

Usually we are testing the question of whether there is any difference between the two means, so $(\mu_1 - \mu_2)$ is usually zero, which simplifies the computation a bit.

Example 5.1.

A diversified company set up separate e-commerce sites to handle orders for two of the company's product lines. Internal auditors randomly selected 32 one-hour periods when they recorded the number of orders placed on site A and 36 periods when they recorded the number of orders place on site B. Summary statistics for the number of orders recorded are as follows:

	Sample Size	Sample Mean	Sample Standard Deviation
Site A	32	31.75	7.8
Site B	36	37	9.7

Assuming equal variances, is there sufficient evidence at the 5% level of significance to conclude that the two sites differ in the average number of orders they generate hourly?

Answer

$H_0: \mu_A - \mu_B = 0$
There is no difference in the average number of orders generated on the two sites.

$H_1: \mu_A - \mu_B \neq 0$
There is a difference in the average number of orders generated on the two sites.

Decision Rule: For $\alpha = 0.05$ and $df = 32 + 36 - 2 = 66$, we will reject the null hypothesis if the calculated test statistic falls above $t = 1.997$ or below $t = -1.997$. See Table 5.1.

Test Statistic: First, compute the pooled variance estimate, then use that estimate to calculate value of the test statistic.

$$s_p^2 = \frac{(n_A - 1) \cdot s_A^2 + (n_B - 1) \cdot s_B^2}{n_A + n_B - 2} = \frac{31 \cdot 7.8^2 + 35 \cdot 9.7^2}{32 + 36 - 2} = 78.5$$

$$t = \frac{(\bar{x}_A - \bar{x}_B) - (\mu_A - \mu_B)}{\sqrt{s_p^2 \cdot \left(\frac{1}{n_A} + \frac{1}{n_B}\right)}} = \frac{(31.75 - 37) - 0}{\sqrt{78.5 \cdot \left(\frac{1}{32} + \frac{1}{36}\right)}} = -2.439$$

Table 5.1. *Finding the Critical Bound in t for df = 66 and 0.025 in One Tail*

The Student's t-Distribution					
α =	0.10	0.05	0.025	0.01	0.005
df = 63	1.295134	1.669402	1.998341	2.387008	2.656145
64	1.29492	1.669013	1.99773	2.386037	2.654854
65	1.294712	1.668636	1.997138	2.385097	2.653604
66	1.294511	1.668271	1.996564	2.384186	2.652393
67	1.294315	1.667916	1.996008	2.383302	2.65122
68	1.294126	1.667572	1.995469	2.382446	2.650081
69	1.293942	1.667239	1.994945	2.381614	2.648977
70	1.293763	1.666914	1.994437	2.380807	2.647905
71	1.293589	1.6666	1.993943	2.380024	2.646863

Observed Significance Level: To find the *p*-value for the *t* test statistic, we use the function in Excel =*tdist(2.439,66,2)*. Note that the *tdist* function of Excel allows us to include the fact that there are 2 tails (the last number in the parentheses), so we do not have to double the area to find a full *p*-value. As an aside, the *tdist* function does not accept negative values for the test statistic, so we need to take the absolute value of $t = -2.439$ as an input to the Excel function.

$$p\text{-value} = 0.0175$$

Conclusion: Since the test statistic of $t = -2.439$ falls well below the lower critical bound of $t = -1.997$, we reject H_0 with at least 95% confidence. Likewise, since the *p*-value of 0.0175 is less than the desired α of 0.05, we reject H_0. There is enough evidence to conclude that the two web sites differ in the average number of orders they generate hourly.

A final note on Example 5.1. is appropriate before we proceed. We may be tempted to conclude that Site A had a smaller average number of orders per hour than Site B. After all, we might rationalize, that is what the sample data say. But we can only speak to the hypothesis that we formed at the beginning of the experiment, which in this case was around the question of whether there was any difference between the two means.

If we overstep our original hypothesis, we will underestimate the risk we have in drawing the final conclusion.

The t-Test for Differences Between Two Means Given Independent Samples and Unequal Variances

When the two populations of interest are nearly normal but we conclude their variances are not equal, differences in their sample means can be approximated by a *t*-distribution, although the degrees of freedom differ from those we used in the equal-variances *t*-test. The calculations for the degrees of freedom to be used in the unequal-variances *t*-test are complex, as shown in the equation that follows, but are easily found in the automated analysis provided routinely by Excel.

t-Test of Two Means Assuming Unequal Variances

$$t = \frac{\text{the sample statistic} - \text{hypothesized difference contained in } H_0}{\text{the standard error of the sample statistic}}$$

$$= \frac{\left(\bar{x}_1 - \bar{x}_2\right) - \left(\mu_1 - \mu_2\right)}{s_{(\bar{x}_1 - \bar{x}_2)}} = \frac{\left(\bar{x}_1 - \bar{x}_2\right) - \left(\mu_1 - \mu_2\right)}{\sqrt{\dfrac{s_1^2}{n_1} + \dfrac{s_2^2}{n_2}}}$$

where n_1 and n_2 are the sample sizes, s_1^2 and s_2^2 are the standard deviations from each of the two samples, and $(\mu_1 - \mu_2)$ is the value shown in H_0. The degrees of freedom against which the test statistic should be compared are given by

$$df = \frac{\left[\dfrac{s_1^2}{n_1} + \dfrac{s_2^2}{n_2}\right]^2}{\dfrac{\left[\dfrac{s_1^2}{n_1}\right]^2}{n_1 - 1} + \dfrac{\left[\dfrac{s_2^2}{n_2}\right]^2}{n_2 - 1}}$$

where we use the integer component of the calculation for *df*, regardless of what value immediately follows the decimal point. For example, calculations of 32.014 and 32.997 would both be rounded down to *df* = 32.

Example 5.2.

A package handler has two offices in the same city. A recent sample of 30 randomly selected customers at the western office indicated that their average wait time for customer service is 5.6 minutes with a standard deviation of 2.24 minutes. During the same time period, a sample of 35 randomly selected customers at the central office indicated that their average wait time for customer service is 7.4 minutes with a standard deviation of 3.78 minutes. Use the unequal variances t-test to determine whether there is any difference in the average wait times for customer service at the two offices. Use $\alpha = 0.05$.

Answer

$H_0: \mu_W - \mu_C = 0$ $H_1: \mu_W - \mu_C \neq 0$

There is no difference in the average wait time for customer service at the two offices.

There is a difference in the average wait time for customer service at the two offices.

Decision Rule: Before we can determine the critical bound in t, we need to compute the degrees of freedom to use in finding the critical bound. Note that the calculation for df uses sample variances, not sample standard deviations.

$$s_W^2 = (2.24)^2 = 5.0176 \qquad\qquad s_C^2 = (3.78)^2 = 14.2884$$

$$df = \frac{\left[\dfrac{s_W^2}{n_W} + \dfrac{s_C^2}{n_C}\right]^2}{\dfrac{\left[\dfrac{s_W^2}{n_W}\right]^2}{n_W - 1} + \dfrac{\left[\dfrac{s_C^2}{n_C}\right]^2}{n_C - 1}} = \frac{\left[\dfrac{5.0176}{30} + \dfrac{14.2884}{35}\right]^2}{\dfrac{\left[\dfrac{5.0176}{30}\right]^2}{29} + \dfrac{\left[\dfrac{14.2884}{35}\right]^2}{34}} = 56.45612$$

So, using only the integer portion of the final answer, we will use $df = 56$. For $\alpha = 0.05$ and $df = 56$, we will reject the null hypothesis if the calculated test statistic falls above $t = 2.003$ or below $t = -2.003$.

Test Statistic:

$$t = \frac{(\bar{x}_W - \bar{x}_C) - (\mu_W - \mu_C)}{\sqrt{\dfrac{s_W^2}{n_W} + \dfrac{s_C^2}{n_C}}} = \frac{(5.6 - 7.4) - 0}{\sqrt{\dfrac{5.0176}{30} + \dfrac{14.2884}{35}}} = -2.37275$$

(We show the full decimal values for the calculations for *df* and the test statistic in case you want to track the calculations yourself.)

Observed Significance Level: To find the *p*-value for the *t* test statistic, we use the function in Excel =*tdist(2.37275,56,2)*.

$$p\text{-value} = 0.0211$$

Conclusion: Since the test statistic of $t = -2.373$ falls well below the lower critical bound of $t = -2.003$, we reject H_0 with at least 95% confidence. Likewise, since the *p*-value of 0.0211 is less than the desired α of 0.05, we reject H_0. There is enough evidence to conclude that there is a difference in the average wait times for customer service at the two offices.

The F-Test for Equality of Two Variances

When we sample randomly from the same population, sample variances do vary simply because we randomly select different subsets of the population. But how different do variances have to be before we are concerned that they are not equal? To test the equality of population variances, whether $\sigma_1^2 = \sigma_2^2$, we form the ratio of the two variances by dividing both sides of the equation by one of the variances. We then determine if the resulting ratio is significantly different from 1. The best estimate for $\left(\sigma_1^2 \big/ \sigma_2^2 \right)$ is the ratio of the two related sample statistics $\left(s_1^2 \big/ s_2^2 \right)$. When two independent samples are taken from normally distributed populations with equal variances, the sampling distribution of their ratios follows an *F*-distribution, named after the English statistician Sir Ronald A. Fisher (1890–1962). The *F*-distribution includes the degrees of freedom for each of the two samples: $n_1 - 1$ degrees of freedom for the numerator and $n_2 - 1$ for the denominator.

quality of Two Variances

$$F = \frac{\text{variance for sample 1}}{\text{variance for sample 2}} = \frac{s_1^2}{s_2^2}$$

. are the numerator degrees of freedom and $n_2 - 1$ are the
freedom associated with the denominator.

ing the upper critical bound for the hypothesis test of the
ɔ is relatively straightforward: find the F-ratio, σ_1^2 / σ_2^2, for $\alpha / 2$
ı $n_1 - 1$ degrees of freedom for the numerator and $n_2 - 1$ degrees
freedom for the denominator. Finding the lower critical bound for
he F-ratio is more complex. Because the F tables were generated under
the assumption that $\sigma_1^2 > \sigma_2^2$, to find the lower critical bound of the
F-ratio, we must switch the degrees of freedom and find the inverse
of the F-ratio, σ_2^2 / σ_1^2, for $\alpha / 2$ that has $n_2 - 1$ degrees of freedom for
the numerator and $n_1 - 1$ degrees of freedom for the denominator.
We often find it more convenient to form the null and alternative
hypotheses with the larger of the two sample variances in the numerator. In doing so, we force the comparison of the F test statistic with
the upper critical bound of the decision rule, which is the easier of the
two bounds to form.

To find the appropriate critical bound from the F-table, we first
determine the amount of area in the upper tail of the desired rejection region. If we are conducting an equality test of variances using
$\alpha = 0.01$, the appropriate table to use shows 0.005 in the upper tail.
If we were conducting an equality test of variances using $\alpha = 0.05$,
then the appropriate table to use shows 0.025 in the upper tail. The
numerator degrees of freedom head the columns across the top of the
table and the denominator degrees of freedom head the rows down
the side of the table. As an example, for numerator $df = 24$, denominator $df = 30$ in an equality test of variances using $\alpha = 0.05$, we
would access the F-table for 0.025 area in the upper tail and find the
$F = 2.14$. See Table 5.2.

Table 5.2. Finding the Critical Bound for a Two-Tailed F-Test With 0.025 in the Upper Tail Given $a = 0.05$, Numerator Degrees of Freedom = 24, and Denominator Degrees of Freedom = 30

Denom df	Num df						
	20	24	30	40	60	120	∞
20	2.46	2.41	2.35	2.29	2.22	2.16	2.09
24	2.33	2.27	2.21	2.15	2.08	2.01	1.94
30	2.20	2.14	2.07	2.01	1.94	1.87	1.79
40	2.07	2.01	1.94	1.88	1.80	1.72	1.64

Example 5.3.

A random sample of recent graduates from an MBA program was asked about their first-year salary after graduation. Responses were separated by gender and summarized:

	Women	Men
Mean	$69,247	$72,154
Standard Deviation	$9,423	$5,242
Count	31	41

Use $\alpha = 0.05$ to determine whether the variance among the women's salaries was significantly different from the variance among the men's salaries.

Answer

$$H_0: \frac{\sigma_W^2}{\sigma_M^2} = 1 \qquad\qquad H_1: \frac{\sigma_W^2}{\sigma_M^2} \neq 1$$

The variances among women's and men's salaries are approximately equal.

The variances among women's and men's salaries are not equal.

Decision Rule: To determine the upper critical bound, we use the numerator $df = 30$, denominator $df = 40$, and $\frac{\alpha}{2} = 0.025$ to find $F = 1.94$. To determine the lower critical bound, we use the numerator $df = 40$, denominator $df = 30$, and $\frac{\alpha}{2} = 0.025$ to find $F = \dfrac{1}{2.01} = 0.498$. So we will reject the null hypothesis if the calculated test statistic falls above $F = 1.943$ or below $F = 0.498$.

Test Statistic:

$$F = \frac{s_W^2}{s_M^2} = \frac{9423^2}{5242^2} = 3.231$$

Observed Significance Level: To find the p-value for the F test statistic, we use the function in Excel $=2*Fdist(3.231,30,40)$. We have to double the output from the *Fdist* function because it assumes a one-tailed test.

$$p\text{-value} = 0.0006$$

Conclusion: Since the test statistic of $F = 3.231$ falls well above the upper critical bound of $F = 1.943$, we reject H_0 with at least 95% confidence. Likewise, since the p-value of 0.0006 is less than the desired α of 0.05, we reject H_0. There is enough evidence to conclude that the variances among women's and men's first-year salaries are not equal. With this result, we would be warranted to use the t-test assuming unequal variances when we test for any difference in the two population means.

The z-Test for Differences Between Two Means Given Independent Samples

In some circumstances, the variances of population parameters are known. Practically speaking, this is true of highly automated processes where the parameters being measured are components of process specifications or where the measurements are taken from a stable historic process. When the population variances are known and the populations themselves are normally distributed, differences in their sample means can be approximated by the standard normal distribution, the z-distribution, regardless of the sizes of the samples taken. When the population variances are known and the sample sizes are sufficiently large, differences in their sample means can be approximated by the standard normal distribution, the z-distribution, regardless of the shapes of the underlying populations.

z-Test of Two Means When Population Variances Are Known

$$z = \frac{\text{the sample statistic} - \text{hypothesized difference contained in } H_0}{\text{the standard error of the sample statistic}}$$

$$= \frac{(\bar{x}_1 - \bar{x}_2) - (\mu_1 - \mu_2)}{\sigma_{(\bar{x}_1 - \bar{x}_2)}} = \frac{(\bar{x}_1 - \bar{x}_2) - (\mu_1 - \mu_2)}{\sqrt{\dfrac{\sigma_1^2}{n_1} + \dfrac{\sigma_2^2}{n_2}}}$$

where σ_1^2 and σ_2^2 are the respective population variances, n_1 and n_2 are the samples sizes, and $(\mu_1 - \mu_2)$ is the difference between the two population means assumed true in the null hypothesis, H_0.

Example 5.4.

A food processor recently expanded production at their base plant in Oakville by adding a new and more technologically advanced fill line. The older line is known to maintain a mean fill of 30 ounces with a standard deviation of 0.026 ounce. The newer line has a mean fill of 30 ounces with a standard deviation of 0.019 ounce. Use the following sample data to determine whether the new line differs in average fill from the older line. Use $\alpha = 0.05$.

	Older Line	New Line
Mean	29.99	30.001
Standard Deviation	0.026	0.019
Count	38	35

Answer

$H_0: \mu_O - \mu_N = 0$ $H_1: \mu_O - \mu_N \neq 0$
There is no difference in the   There is a difference in the
average product weight for   average product weight for
the two fill lines.   the two fill lines.

Decision Rule: For $\alpha = 0.05$, we will reject the null hypothesis if the calculated test statistic falls above $z = 1.96$ or below $z = -1.96$.

Test Statistic:

$$z = \frac{(\bar{x}_O - \bar{x}_N) - (\mu_O - \mu_N)}{\sigma_{(\bar{x}_O - \bar{x}_N)}} = \frac{(\bar{x}_O - \bar{x}_N) - (\mu_O - \mu_N)}{\sqrt{\frac{\sigma_O^2}{n_O} + \frac{\sigma_N^2}{n_N}}} = \frac{29.99 - 30.001}{\sqrt{\frac{.026^2}{38} + \frac{.019^2}{35}}} = -2.07$$

Observed Significance Level:

$$p\text{-value} = 2(0.0197) = 0.0384$$

Conclusion: Since the test statistic of $z = -2.07$ falls below the critical bounds of $z = -1.96$, we reject H_0 with at least 95% confidence. Likewise, since the p-value of 0.0384 is less than the desired α of 0.05, we reject H_0. There is enough evidence to conclude that the two fill lines have a different average product weight.

The *t*-Test for Differences Between Two Means Given Dependent Samples

Selecting pairs of similar elements and then submitting each of the pair to different experimental treatments is one of the most powerful research designs available. When facing a difficult decision, who wouldn't love to identify a pair of clones and send each on different paths into the future to know which path had the better outcome? The analysis of matched pairs is a powerful design for the very reason that the researcher is able to hold all other characteristics constant and focus solely on the effect of the different treatments.

As we have seen in prior sections of this chapter, the comparison of independent samples assumes that the samples are randomly selected and represent the heterogeneity inherent in each of the two populations. Because they are randomly selected, the samples, in essence, are little microcosms of each of the underlying populations. In contrast, dependent samples represent a random sample from one population but a controlled sample from a second population. Once the sample is selected from the first population, elements included in the second sample are in some way either dictated or constrained by the identity of the elements in the first sample. The design of the research plan for two means given dependent samples is itself made more complex by the process required to identify matched pairs of elements, or "clones."

The process of matching elements from one population with elements selected from another population is difficult when such twins do not occur naturally. Pairing observations taken from the same individual before and after a treatment is among the simpler designs using dependent samples. Matching pairs can be both extensive and invasive if the design requires, for example, genetic or psychological profiles of central characteristics. Of essence in the identification of matched pairs is the fact that elements in a second sample are selected precisely because they mirror elements in the first sample. The samples are in no way independent of one another.

Not only is the research design for matched pairs different from that used in identifying independent samples, but the analysis of the results also differs from what we have seen in prior sections of this chapter. In matching the pairs of observations, we analyze the differences observed across each pair by forming the mean and standard deviation of the differences noted for each paired set of observations. As long as the populations being sampled are approximately normally distributed, analysis of the average difference then closely tracks the t-test conducted on one-population parameters as performed in Chapter 4.

There is an important toll paid for designing a paired difference analysis as opposed to an analysis of two independently selected samples: the degrees of freedom on the associated t-statistic are half the size of the degrees of freedom for independently selected samples. Note that the degrees of freedom for a t-test for the mean difference of two dependent samples is the number of pairs of observations minus one rather than the independent sample sizes added together minus two. In exchange for the loss of degrees of freedom, however, the successful paired differences t-test reduces sources of fluctuation that occur from extraneous influences within the variable being measured and focuses the standard error on the differences between the paired observations.

> ### t-Test for Difference in Two Means for Dependent Samples
>
> $$t = \frac{\text{a sample mean} - \text{the hypothesized value}}{\text{the standard error}} = \frac{\bar{x}_D - \mu}{s_D \big/ \sqrt{n_D}}$$
>
> where $\bar{x}_D$, s_D and n_D are values associated with the differences between the pairs of observations, $df = n_D - 1$, and the hypothesized value for μ is specified in the null hypothesis, H_0.

Example 5.5.

Before releasing an advertisement for a new product, the advertising executive for a major fast food chain planned to collect sales data from 25 franchises in the region to track the effectiveness of the new campaign. He selected two dates, one before release and one after release of the advertisement, and requested daily sales totals from each of the 25 outlets. Summary statistics are as follows:

$$\bar{x}_D = \$52.48 \qquad\qquad s_D = \$132.5378$$

Assuming the populations sampled are approximately normally distributed, is there sufficient evidence to show that the new campaign was effective in increasing the daily sales revenues for franchises in the restaurant chain? Use $\alpha = 0.05$.

Answer

$H_0: \mu_{After} - \mu_{Before}{}^* \leq 0$

The new advertising campaign was not effective in increasing the daily sales revenues for franchises in the chain.

$H_1: \mu_{After} - \mu_{Before}{}^* > 0$

The new advertising campaign was effective in increasing the daily sales revenues for franchises in the chain.

*Instead of using a single expression, μ_D, to refer to the difference, we show the expression $(\mu_{After} - \mu_{Before})$ to indicate the order in which the difference was calculated. To be clear, $(\mu_{After} - \mu_{Before}) = \mu_D$.

Decision Rule: For $\alpha = 0.05$ and $df = 25 - 1 = 24$, we will reject the null hypothesis if the calculated test statistic falls above $t = 1.711$.

Test Statistic:

$$t = \frac{\overline{x}_D - \mu}{s_D / \sqrt{n_D}} = \frac{52.48}{132.5378 / \sqrt{25}} = 1.9798$$

Observed Significance Level: To find the p-value for the t test statistic, we use the function in Excel $=tdist(1.9798,24,1)$.

$$p\text{-value} = 0.02965$$

Conclusion: Since the test statistic of $t = 1.9798$ falls above the critical bound of $t = 1.1711$, we reject H_0 with at least 95% confidence. Likewise, since the p-value of 0.02965 is less than the desired α of 0.05, we reject H_0. There is enough evidence to conclude that the new advertising campaign is effective in increasing the daily sales revenues for franchises in the chain.

The z-Test for Differences Between Two Proportions

As municipal, state, and national election polls predict popular support for favored candidates and causes, the estimation and comparison of population proportions play an important role in anticipating and expressing the voice of the people and their democratic decisions. Preelection polls boast support for this or that candidate or cause at a certain level, within plus or minus a stated percent. There are few statistical topics as widely publicized or as important to the conduct of political processes as the estimation and comparison of population proportions. The difference between two population proportions plays an equally important role in business, in market research, business forecasting, financial auditing, and analysis of comparative defect rates, to name a few. At the heart of the proportion is a count, not a measurement, of sampled elements. When we sort a sample into subgroups—those elements that do meet a certain criterion and those that do not—and then produce a count of these subgroups, we use a proportion to compare the results.

Inferences about $(p_1 - p_2)$ are based on two random samples from two unrelated populations. The two samples do not have to be the same size. We summarize the sample statistics for each, including sample sizes, the number of successes in each sample, and the sample proportions. The best estimate for the population parameter $(p_1 - p_2)$ is the sample statistic $(\bar{p}_1 - \bar{p}_2)$, where p_1 is the proportion for population 1, p_2 is the proportion for population 2, $\bar{p}_1 = \dfrac{x_1}{n_1}$ is the proportion for sample 1, and $\bar{p}_2 = \dfrac{x_2}{n_2}$ is the proportion for sample 2. Since we assume the population proportions are equal in the null hypothesis, we combine the two samples and form a single pooled estimate of the population proportion, $\bar{p}_{pooled} = \dfrac{x_1 + x_2}{n_1 + n_2}$, which we use in the calculation of the test statistic, if the sample sizes are sufficiently large.

If the sample sizes are sufficiently large, the sampling distribution of $(\bar{p}_1 - \bar{p}_2)$ can be approximated by the standard normal, or z, distribution. As with the considerations for a single population proportion, what constitutes "sufficiently large" depends on both the size of the sample and the proportion of its population that satisfies the characteristic of interest. In the case of two population proportions, all four computations must generate a minimum expected count of 5: $n_1 \cdot \bar{p} \geq 5$, $n_1 \cdot (1 - \bar{p}_1) \geq 5$, $n_2 \cdot \bar{p}_2 \geq 5$, $n_2 \cdot (1 - \bar{p}_2) \geq 5$.

---

z-Test of Two Proportions When Sample Sizes Are Sufficiently Large for H_0: $p_1 - p_2$ {=, ≥, ≤} 0

$$z = \frac{\text{the sample statistic} - \text{hypothesized difference contained in } H_0}{\text{the standard error of the sample statistic}}$$

$$= \frac{(\bar{p}_1 - \bar{p}_2) - (p_1 - p_2)}{\sigma_{(\bar{p}_1 - \bar{p}_2)}} = \frac{(\bar{p}_1 - \bar{p}_2) - 0}{\sqrt{\bar{p}_{pooled}(1 - \bar{p}_{pooled})\left(\dfrac{1}{n_1} + \dfrac{1}{n_2}\right)}}$$

where the difference between the two population proportions is zero, which is assumed true in the null hypothesis, H_0.

Example 5.6.

A local baking company is testing some new cracker recipes. Their goal is to deliver boxes of crackers that pass consumer taste tests but have no broken crackers after shipping. From taste tests, the bakers narrowed the competition to two recipes, A and B. Bakers then produced each recipe, boxed the crackers, and loaded them onto delivery trucks. Drivers were told to take the boxes on the normal route but to deliver them back to the bakery at the end of their route rather than off-load them at consumer outlets. Once returned, the boxes were opened and inspected. A box with no broken crackers was scored a "0" and a box with one or more broken was scored a "1." Results are as follows:

	Recipe A	Recipe B
x, Number of Defects	9	5
n, Number Sampled	30	40
Sample Proportions	0.3	0.125

Use a 95% level of confidence to determine whether there is any difference in the proportion of broken crackers for Recipes A and B.

Answer

$H_0: p_A - p_B = 0$

There is no difference in the proportion of broken crackers for Recipes A and B.

$H_1: p_A - p_B \neq 0$

There is a difference in the proportion of broken crackers for Recipes A and B.

Decision Rule: For $\alpha = 0.05$, we will reject the null hypothesis if the calculated test statistic falls above $z = 1.96$ or below $z = -1.96$.

Test Statistic:

First we must compute $\bar{P}_{pooled} = \dfrac{x_A + x_B}{n_A + n_B} = \dfrac{9 + 5}{30 + 40} = 0.2$

$$z = \dfrac{(\bar{P}_A - \bar{P}_B) - (p_A - p_B)}{\sqrt{\bar{P}_{pooled}(1 - \bar{P}_{pooled})\left(\dfrac{1}{n_A} + \dfrac{1}{n_B}\right)}} = \dfrac{(0.3 - 0.125) - 0}{\sqrt{0.2 \cdot (1 - 0.2) \cdot \left(\dfrac{1}{30} + \dfrac{1}{40}\right)}} = 1.81$$

Observed Significance Level: p-value = 2*(0.0351) = 0.0702

Conclusion: Since the test statistic of $z = 1.81$ falls between the critical bounds of $z = \pm 1.96$, we do not reject H_0 with at least 95% confidence. Likewise, since the p-value of 0.0702 is greater than the desired α of 0.05, we do not reject H_0. There is not enough evidence to conclude that the proportion of broken crackers differs for Recipes A and B.

Using Excel to Conduct Analyses of Two Population Means and Variances

Descriptive statistics are needed to conduct the analyses we have done to date: sample means, standard deviations, and counts. If the descriptive statistics are not already given for a set of data, Excel can easily derive the values. In Chapter 4, we referenced the individual functions embedded in Excel for each of the descriptive statistics. Excel also has some programmed capabilities that make the comparatively complex calculations involving the analysis of two or more populations much easier. We can access them through the toolbar in the Data ribbon under the specific button for Data Analysis. If your computer does not show the Data Analysis capability, you can update the application by going to the Windows button and installing the toolkit over the web for later versions of Excel.

Using the Data Analysis toolkit, we can access several powerful programmed functions. Of interest to us in this chapter are the following:

- Descriptive Statistics
- *F*-Test Two Sample for Variances
- *t*-Test: Assuming Equal Variances
- *t*-Test: Assuming Unequal Variances
- *t*-Test: Paired Two Sample for Means
- *z*-Test: Two Sample for Means

All of these imbedded programs require the actual data list from each sample, as opposed to summary statistics from each sample. A brief description of each follows.

Descriptive Statistics

To access this Excel program, activate the Data Analysis toolkit on the spreadsheet with the data list and select this program. Enter the range of the data for which you want summary statistics. If a label for the data list heads the column or row of data, include the label and check the box confirming the label is in the first row or column, depending on the orientation of your data. Toward the bottom of the window, click "Summary Statistics." Click the output range and activate the field by clicking your mouse in that field. Identify a single cell where the beginning of the output should be placed on your spreadsheet. Click "OK" at the top of the box. Output will include, among others, the mean, the standard deviation, the variance, and the count. It is always wise to double check that the count in the output matches the count of values you know to be included in the data list to verify you included the entire list.

F-Test: Two Sample for Variances

To access this Excel program, activate the Data Analysis toolkit on the spreadsheet with the data list and select this program. Enter the range of the data you want for the numerator variable as Variable 1 and the data you want for the denominator variable as Variable 2. If a label for the data list heads the column or row of data, include the label and check the box confirming the label is in the first row or column, depending on the orientation of your data. Since the F-test for the equality of two variances is a two-tailed test, report $\alpha/_2$ as the value in the field labeled "Alpha." Click the output range and activate the field by clicking your mouse in that field. Identify a single cell where the beginning of the output should be placed on your spreadsheet. Click "OK" at the top of the box. Output will include means, variances, counts, df, the calculated test statistic, the one-tailed p-value, and the upper critical bound. Don't forget that you need to double the reported one-tailed p-value to get the full two-tailed p-value.

t-Test: Assuming Equal Variances

To access this Excel program, activate the Data Analysis toolkit on the spreadsheet with the data list and select this program. Enter the range of the data you want for the first variable as Variable 1 and the data you want for the second variable, which is shown as subtracted from Variable 1 in H_0, as Variable 2. If a label for the data list heads the column or row of data, include the label and check the box confirming the label is in the first row or column, depending on the orientation of your data. Enter the full α shown in the hypothesis test in the field labeled "Alpha." Click the output range and activate the field by clicking your mouse in that field. Identify a single cell where the beginning of the output should be placed on your spreadsheet. Click "OK" at the top of the box. Output will include means, variances, counts, pooled variance, df, the calculated test statistic, the one-tailed and two-tailed p-values, and the upper critical bound for both a one-tailed and a two-tailed hypothesis test. If your test has a lower-tail rejection region, you need to take the negative of the upper critical bound to find the lower critical bound that is the boundary value for the rejection region.

t-Test: Assuming Unequal Variances

To access this Excel program, activate the Data Analysis toolkit on the spreadsheet with the data list and select this program. Enter the range of the data you want for the first variable as Variable 1 and the data you want for the second variable, which is shown as subtracted from Variable 1 in H_0, as Variable 2. If a label for the data list heads the column or row of data, include the label and check the box confirming the label is in the first row or column, depending on the orientation of your data. Enter the full α shown in the hypothesis test in the field labeled "Alpha." Click the output range and activate the field by clicking your mouse in that field. Identify a single cell where the beginning of the output should be placed on your spreadsheet. Click "OK" at the top of the box. Output will include means, variances, counts, df, the calculated test statistic, the one-tailed and two-tailed p-values, and the upper critical bound for both a one-tailed and a two-tailed hypothesis test. If your test has a lower-tail rejection region, you need to take the negative of the upper critical bound to find the lower critical bound that is the boundary value for the rejection region.

t-Test: Paired Two Sample for Means

To access this Excel program, activate the Data Analysis toolkit on the spreadsheet with the data list and select this program. Enter the range of the data you want for the first variable as Variable 1 and the data you want for the second variable, which is shown as subtracted from Variable 1 in H_0, as Variable 2. If a label for the data list heads the column or row of data, include the label and check the box confirming the label is in the first row or column, depending on the orientation of your data. Enter the full α shown in the hypothesis test in the field labeled "Alpha." Click the output range and activate the field by clicking your mouse in that field. Identify a single cell where the beginning of the output should be placed on your spreadsheet. Click "OK" at the top of the box. Output will include means, variances, counts, *df*, the calculated test statistic, the one-tailed and two-tailed *p*-values, and the upper critical bound for both a one-tailed and a two-tailed hypothesis test. If your test has a lower-tail rejection region, you need to take the negative of the upper critical bound to find the lower critical bound that is the boundary value for the rejection region.

z-Test: Two Sample for Means

To access this Excel program, activate the Data Analysis toolkit on the spreadsheet with the data list and select this program. Enter the range of the data you want for the first variable as Variable 1 and the data you want for the second variable, which is shown as subtracted from Variable 1 in H_0, as Variable 2. If a label for the data list heads the column or row of data, include the label and check the box confirming the label is in the first row or column, depending on the orientation of your data. Enter the values for each of the known variances. Enter the full α shown in the hypothesis test in the field labeled "Alpha." Click the output range and activate the field by clicking your mouse in that field. Identify a single cell where the beginning of the output should be placed on your spreadsheet. Click "OK" at the top of the box. Output will include means, variances, counts, *df*, the calculated test statistic, the one-tailed and two-tailed *p*-values, and the upper critical bound for both a one-tailed and a two-tailed hypothesis test. If your test has a lower-tail rejection region, you need to take the negative of the upper critical bound to find the lower critical bound that is the boundary value for the rejection region.

Confidence Intervals on the Difference of Means From Two Populations, Independent Samples

Rather than test whether two population means differ, we may want to estimate how different the two means are. When samples are taken randomly from two normally distributed populations with equal variances, the sampling distribution of their difference follows a t-distribution with $n_1 + n_2 - 2$ degrees of freedom. So, $100(1 - \alpha)\%$ of the samples taken will have a difference that falls within the interval defined by the sample statistic $\pm\ t_{a/2} \cdot$ the standard error of the sample statistic. When we estimate the difference between two means taken from populations with approximately equal variances, the confidence interval is found with the equation $(\overline{x}_1 - \overline{x}_2) \pm t \cdot s_{(\overline{x}_1 - \overline{x}_2)} = (\overline{x}_1 - \overline{x}_2) \pm t \cdot \sqrt{s_p^2 \cdot \left(\dfrac{1}{n_1} + \dfrac{1}{n_2}\right)}$ where the pooled variance, s_p^2, is defined by the equation we introduced early in this chapter, $s_p^2 = \dfrac{(n_1 - 1) \cdot s_1^2 + (n_2 - 1) \cdot s_2^2}{n_1 + n_2 - 2}$.

Example 5.7.

Holiday shopping accounts for a significant portion of retail sales in the United States. A random sample of 35 households was examined to determine last year's holiday spending. An earlier random sample of 37 households was similarly examined for the prior year. The results are summarized in the following table. Assuming the populations are approximately normally distributed, use a 95% confidence level to determine the upper and lower bounds on the difference in average household holiday spending between the two years.

	Last Year	The Year Before
Mean	$704.97	$652.87
Standard Deviation	$296.59	$262.66
Count	35	37

Answer

Because the populations are approximately normally distributed and the sample sizes sufficiently large, we will use a t-confidence interval to establish bounds on the difference in average household holiday spending between the two years. To be 95% confident, the 5% risk we are wrong is split between the upper and lower tails of the distribution. The appropriate t-coefficient is $t = \pm 1.994$.

Pooled variance estimate:

$$s_p^2 = \frac{s_1^2 \cdot (n_1 - 1) + s_2^2 \cdot (n_2 - 1)}{n_1 + n_2 - 2} = \frac{296.59^2 \cdot 34 + 265.53^2 \cdot 36}{70} = 78986.48$$

Upper bound:

$$(\bar{x}_1 - \bar{x}_2) + t \cdot \sqrt{s_p^2 \cdot \left(\frac{1}{n_1} + \frac{1}{n_2}\right)} = (704.97 - 656.08) + 1.994 \cdot \sqrt{78986.48 \cdot \left(\frac{1}{35} + \frac{1}{37}\right)}$$

$$= 48.89 + 132.14 = 181.03$$

Lower bound:

$$(\bar{x}_1 - \bar{x}_2) - t \cdot \sqrt{s_p^2 \cdot \left(\frac{1}{n_1} + \frac{1}{n_2}\right)} = (704.97 - 656.08) - 1.994 \cdot \sqrt{78986.48 \cdot \left(\frac{1}{35} + \frac{1}{37}\right)}$$

$$= 48.89 - 132.14 = -83.25$$

Interpretation: Approximately 95% of the time we take samples of 35 and 37 households from the two years under study, we will find a difference in their average household holiday spending of between −$83.25 and $181.03. Since zero is in the calculated interval, we cannot be certain with 95% confidence that there is any real difference in the average household holiday spending between the two years.

Confidence Intervals on the Difference of Proportions From Two Populations

When sample sizes are sufficiently large, the sampling distribution of the difference in their proportions follows the z-distribution. So, $100(1 - \alpha)\%$ of the samples taken will have a difference that falls within the interval defined by the sample statistic $\pm\, z_{\alpha/2} \cdot$ the standard error of the sample statistic.

When we estimate the difference between two proportions, the confidence interval is found with the equation

$$(\bar{p}_1 - \bar{p}_2) \pm z \cdot \sigma_{(\bar{p}_1 - \bar{p}_2)} = (\bar{p}_1 - \bar{p}_2) \pm z \cdot \sqrt{\frac{\bar{p}_1 \cdot (1 - \bar{p}_1)}{n_1} + \frac{\bar{p}_2 \cdot (1 - \bar{p}_2)}{n_2}}$$

In calculating the standard error for the confidence interval on the difference of two proportions, note that we do not use the pooled estimate of the population proportion, $\bar{p}_{pooled}$, as we did in calculating the standard error for the test statistic used in the hypothesis test. We do not use the pooled estimate of the population proportion here because we have not assumed the two population proportions are equal as we did in the null hypothesis of the hypothesis test.

Example 5.8.

Employee sick leave rates are monitored at two manufacturing sites, one located in Denver, Colorado and the other in Kansas City, Missouri. A random sample of 80 Denver employees noted 8 had called in sick for one or more days in the first quarter of the year. In comparison, a random sample of 100 Kansas City employees found 6 had called in sick one or more days in the first quarter of operation there. Use a 95% confidence level to determine the upper and lower bounds on the difference in the proportion of employees calling in sick at the two plants.

Answer

Because the numbers of employees utilizing sick leave are both greater than 5, the samples are sufficiently large to calculate a z-confidence interval on the difference of the two proportions.

$$(\bar{p}_1 - \bar{p}_2) \pm z \cdot \sqrt{\frac{\bar{p}_1 \cdot (1 - \bar{p}_1)}{n_1} + \frac{\bar{p}_2 \cdot (1 - \bar{p}_2)}{n_2}} = (0.10 - 0.06) \pm 1.96 \cdot \sqrt{\frac{0.10 \cdot 0.90}{80} + \frac{0.06 \cdot 0.94}{100}}$$

$$= 0.04 \pm 0.08055$$

Lower bound = −0.04055, Upper bound = 0.12055

Interpretation: Approximately 95% of the time we take samples of 80 and 100 employees from the two manufacturing sites, we will find a difference in their employee sick leave rates of between −4.1% and 12.1%. Since zero is in the calculated interval, we cannot be certain with 95% confidence that there is any real difference in the employee sick leave rates at the two sites.

CHAPTER 6

Analysis of Variance From Two or More Populations

In prior chapters, we explored the analysis of numerical data from one and two populations. This chapter expands our discussion of population means to accommodate the simultaneous analysis of multiple populations. With the increased complexity of multiple populations, we may find common attributes that cross the populations of interest and affect the variable we want to study. In such circumstances, appropriate design of the experiment generating the data to be analyzed becomes essential. More than other chapters, then, this chapter focuses on the experimental design leading to data collection for analysis. We will continue our discussion of means and variances of numerical data, but we will develop analytic tools to compare multiple population means with a new capability to identify and account for the effect of a confounding variable. We will continue to use sample statistics, standard errors, and acceptable levels of significance in calculating test statistics. All *F*-tests in analysis of variance are conducted as one-tailed tests.

The Design of Experiments

In our review of analysis of variance, shortened to the acronym ANOVA, we will consider three basic experimental designs: single factor, two-factor without replication, and two-factor with replication. The analyses differ not in the kind of data gathered but the way in which the data are gathered.

In single factor ANOVA, also referred to as one-way ANOVA, a single variable is measured for random samples taken from multiple populations. The data are grouped as samples from each of the populations of interest. The number of groups in the data represent the number of populations sampled, which is also the number of levels of the factor being analyzed. If, for example, we are interested in the lengths of time to complete an athletic event for participating athletes from five different age groups, then each athlete's time to completion is the variable being measured and the measurements will be sorted into one of the five different age groups. Age is the factor being analyzed. This ANOVA has five levels of the single factor, age. The analysis of completion times will seek to determine whether the average completion time differs across the five different age groups. Because we want to see completion times change as a function of age groups, in this example, age is an independent variable and time to completion is the dependent variable. The analysis can accommodate different numbers of sampled elements at each of the factor levels—that is, we would not have to sample the same number of athletes in each age group.

In two-factor ANOVA without replication, a single numerical variable generates data from multiple populations. Elements are sampled from each of the populations of interest. But a second classification cuts across the multiple populations, creating a grid that guides our selection of population elements in a specific way. We randomly sample a single element from each of the multiple populations that represents each of the levels of the second classification. So, for example, if we are interested in the lengths of time to complete an athletic event and we have five different age groups, but we suspect an athlete's weight may affect the recorded completion times, we can use ANOVA to separate the effects of age groups and weight classes on the dependent variable, time to completion. Let us assume for this example that four different weight categories are identified. In two-factor ANOVA without replication, we would sample a total of 20 athletes, one athlete at each of the four weight categories within each of the five age groups. Again we would record each athlete's time to completion as the variable being measured, and the measurements would be carefully placed in each cell of the data grid. The analysis of completion times can determine whether the average completion time differs across the five different age groups, as well as whether average completion time differs across the four different weight classes. In this example, both age and weight are independent variables and completion time is the dependent variable. The number of elements sampled is restricted to the product of the number of levels for the two independent variables, age and weight.

Two-factor ANOVA with replication is designed similarly to two-factor ANOVA without replication, with the exception that we have multiple elements for each combination of categories for the independent variables. For the problems we will deal with in this chapter, the number of elements in each cell must be the same, so the total elements sampled must be some multiple times the number of cells in the data grid. If, to continue our example, we have five age groups and four weight classes, for two-factor ANOVA with replication we would then plan to sample 40 athletes or 60 athletes or 80 athletes, and so on, where the number of replications is the number of athletes sampled for each cell of the age-weight class data grid. With two-factor ANOVA with replication, we can test for the interactive effects of age and weight classes. Such results might show that older and heavier athletes perform differently than younger and lighter athletes. If interaction effects are not significant, the analyst can then test for the individual main effects of age and weight.

Single-Factor ANOVA: The Completely Randomized Design

Single-factor ANOVA is the simplest of the experimental designs used in ANOVA. While it can be used to analyze differences in two population means, its strength is best shown in testing differences among means from three or more populations. In one light, elements sampled for single-factor ANOVA can be seen as members of a single, broad population, who are randomly assigned to different treatment groups and, following treatment, are then measured on some dimension to determine the effect of each treatment. For example, the tensile strength of rope woven three different ways from the same fiber source can be compared to determine if the weaving introduces different average strength to one rope than to the others. In another light, single-factor ANOVA can be viewed as a tool to analyze a single variable as it exists within distinctly different populations. For example, the tensile strength of ropes woven the same way from different fiber sources can be compared to determine if the average strength of one rope woven from one fiber differs from the average strength of ropes woven from other fibers. Both applications of single-factor ANOVA are appropriate. To conduct single-factor ANOVA, the dependent variable must be approximately normally distributed in each of the populations sampled and the variances of the dependent variable must be approximately equal in each of the populations.

The single-factor analysis of variance is based on the sum of squared differences between individual data values and their group and grand means. The total variation is formed by the sum of the squared differences between all elements sampled and the grand mean of the sampled elements regardless of what group or level they are assigned to or represent. The total variation is parsed into between-groups variation (variation that is *explained* by an element's membership in a particular group) and within-groups variation (variation that is *unexplained* by an element's group membership). Mathematically, we can summarize these relationships with the following equations:

Single-Factor ANOVA of c Different Means,
$$H_0: \mu_1 = \mu_2 = \ldots = \mu_c$$

Variations:

$$\textbf{Total: } SS(\text{Total}) = \sum_{j=1}^{c} \sum_{i=1}^{n} \left(x_{ij} - \bar{\bar{x}} \right)^2$$

This is the total fluctuation represented among all data values sampled.

$$\textbf{Between-Groups: } SS(\text{Treatment}) = \sum_{j=1}^{c} n_j \cdot \left(\bar{x}_j - \bar{\bar{x}} \right)^2$$

This is the fluctuation between group means and the grand mean weighted by the number of elements within each group. It represents the fluctuation that is *explained* by group identity.

$$\textbf{Within-Groups: } SS(\text{Error}) = \sum_{j=1}^{c} \sum_{i=1}^{n} \left(x_{ij} - \bar{x}_j \right)^2$$

This is the fluctuation between group elements and that group's mean. It represents the fluctuation that is *unexplained* by group identity.

where

c = the number of groups or levels of the independent variable,

n_j = the number of elements sampled in a given group,

$\bar{\bar{x}}$ = the grand mean of all elements sampled regardless of what group they are in, and

$\bar{x}_j$ = the group mean for elements sampled in group j.

$$SS(\text{Total}) = SS(\text{Treatment}) + SS(\text{Error})$$

Table 6.1. *Single-Factor ANOVA*

Source of Variation	SS	df	MS	F	p-Value	F Crit
Treatment	$SSTR = \sum_{j=1}^{c} n_j (\bar{x}_j - \bar{\bar{x}})^2$	$c-1$	$MSTR = \dfrac{SSTR}{c-1}$	$F = \dfrac{MSTR}{MSE}$	"=FDIST$(F_{,c-1,n-c})$"	"=FINV$(\alpha,c-1,n-c)$"
Error	$SSE = \sum_{j=1}^{c}\sum_{i=1}^{n_j} (x_{ij} - \bar{x}_j)^2$	$n-c$	$MSE = \dfrac{SSE}{n-c}$			
Total	$SST = \sum_{j=1}^{c}\sum_{i=1}^{n_j} (x_{ij} - \bar{\bar{x}})^2$	$n-1$				

Variation must be converted to variance before we can begin to discuss conducting tests of hypotheses, because it is the *ratio of variances*, as we saw in the prior chapter, that leads to the *F*-test. To form variance, the sum of squares (*SS*) is divided by its degrees of freedom, forming the column headed by MS in Table 6.1.

The *F*-statistic is formed by the ratio of the between-groups variance divided by the within-groups variance. A large between-groups variance and a small within-groups variance lead to a large *F*-statistic. The larger the *F*-statistic is, the smaller its *p*-Value and the more likely we are to reject the null hypothesis, which is our objective in structuring a hypothesis test in the first place. The degrees of freedom for the *F*-statistic are given by the degrees of freedom on the numerator and the denominator—that is, $(c - 1)$ for the numerator and $(n - c)$ for the denominator. Although the equations to perform the analysis by hand are given in Table 6.1, Excel's Data Analysis toolkit has a menu choice that will automate the analysis of raw data, which we use here.

Example 6.1.

An experimental project was run in mature navel orange orchards in Central California managed by three different companies. The number of fancy grade fruit produced by trees in each of their orchards were sampled and recorded for the last year. Assume the number of fruit is approximately normally distributed and the sampled trees were randomly and independently selected. Use the Excel printout shown in Table 6.2 to determine whether there is evidence at the 5% level of significance of a difference in the average number of fruit produced in the three orchards.

Answer

$$H_0: \mu_A = \mu_B = \mu_C \qquad H_1: \text{At least one of the means}$$
$$\text{differs from the rest.}$$

Decision Rule: For $\alpha = 0.05$ with numerator $df = 2$ and denominator $df = 81$, we will reject the null hypothesis if the calculated test statistic falls above $F = 3.109$.

Table 6.2. Single-Factor ANOVA

SUMMARY

Groups	Count	Sum	Average	Variance
A: Pacific SunTreat	31	16611	535.8387	2217.206
B: Western Navel Co-op	25	14093	563.72	1324.877
C: Central California Citrus	28	15069	538.1786	1618.374

ANOVA

Source of Variation	SS	df	MS	F	P-value	F crit
Between Groups	12665.08	2	6332.538	3.611985	0.031433	3.109307
Within Groups	142009.3	81	1753.202			
Total	154674.4	83				

Test Statistic:

$$F = \frac{MS(Between\ Groups)}{MS(Within\ Groups)} = \frac{6332.538}{1753.202} = 3.612$$

Observed Significance Level:

$$p\text{-value} = 0.031$$

Conclusion: Since the test statistic of $F = 3.612$ falls above the critical bound of $F = 3.109$, we reject H_0 with at least 95% confidence. Likewise, since the p-value of 0.031 is less than the desired α of 0.05, we reject H_0. There is enough evidence to conclude that at least one of the orchards achieved a different average production than the other two orchards.

Two-Factor ANOVA Without Replication: The Randomized Block Design With One Observation in Each Cell

Two-factor ANOVA without replication allows us to add a second dimension to the comparison of means across treatment groups accomplished in single-factor ANOVA. This analysis assumes the two dimensions are independent of one another. Like single-factor ANOVA, two-factor ANOVA without replication is an additive model in that the total sum of squares is parsed between explained variation and unexplained variation. By adding a second factor to the experimental design, two-factor ANOVA without replication allows us to account for additional fluctuation in the dependent variable that we suspect is associated with a second variable but that is not fully explained by the primary variable. In adding a second factor to the analysis, we further reduce the unexplained within-group variation, SS(Error), which in turn, which leads to a smaller mean square error (MSE) in the denominator to the F-statistic, and a stronger test result.

While single-factor ANOVA allows groups of varying sample sizes, the addition of a second variable in two-factor ANOVA creates a data grid that confines and prescribes the sampling design the researcher using two-factor ANOVA without replication must follow. Specifically, if there are r levels in the row variable and c levels in the column variable, then the data grid across which the sampled elements are recorded is r by c with $n = (r \cdot c)$ total number of cells. This new sampling design requires one sampled element for each cell.

Two-Factor ANOVA Without Replication

Row variable: $H_0: \mu_1 = \mu_2 = \ldots \mu_r$ **Column variable:** $H_0: \mu_1 = \mu_2 = \ldots \mu_c$

Variations:

$$\textbf{Total: } SS(\text{Total}) = \sum_{i=1}^{r} \sum_{j=1}^{c} \left(x_{ij} - \bar{\bar{x}} \right)^2$$

This is the total fluctuation represented among all data values sampled.

$$\textbf{Between-Rows Effect: } SS(\text{Row}) = c \cdot \sum_{i=1}^{r} \left(\bar{x}_i - \bar{\bar{x}} \right)^2$$

This is the fluctuation between row means and the grand mean weighted by c, the number of elements within each row. It represents the fluctuation that is *explained* by row identity.

$$\textbf{Between-Columns Effect: } SS(\text{Column}) = r \cdot \sum_{j=1}^{c} \left(\bar{x}_j - \bar{\bar{x}} \right)^2$$

This is the fluctuation between column means and the grand mean weighted by r, the number of elements within each column. It represents the fluctuation that is *explained* by column identity.

$$\textbf{Within-Groups Effect: } SS(\text{Error}) = \sum_{i=1}^{r} \sum_{j=1}^{c} \left(x_{ij} - \bar{x}_i - \bar{x}_j + \bar{\bar{x}} \right)^2$$

This is the fluctuation that is *unexplained* by row or column identity.

where

> c = the number of groups or levels of the independent column variable,
>
> r = the number of groups or levels of the independent row variable,
>
> $\bar{\bar{x}}$ = the grand mean of all elements sampled regardless of what group they are in,
>
> $\bar{x}_j$ = the group mean for elements sampled in column group j,
>
> $\bar{x}_i$ = the group mean for elements sampled in row group i, and
>
> x_{ij} = the individual data value reported in the ith row and the jth column.
>
> $$SS(\text{Total}) = SS(\text{Row}) + SS(\text{Column}) + SS(\text{Error})$$

Example 6.2.

To examine the heights in inches of three different varieties of pepper plants, an experimental project was run on four plots with different soil types. Assume plant heights are approximately normally distributed. Use the Excel printout shown in Table 6.3 to determine whether there is evidence at the 5% level of significance of a difference in the average heights of plants by soil plot and by seed variety.

Answer: Testing Across Soil Plots

Table 6.3. Two-Factor ANOVA Without Replication

Anova: Two-Factor Without Replication

SUMMARY	Count	Sum	Average	Variance
Plot 1	3	41.6	13.86667	1.003333
Plot 2	3	41.8	13.93333	2.263333
Plot 3	3	43.9	14.63333	1.843333
Plot 4	3	49.2	16.4	2.47
Seed A	4	55.2	13.8	2.78
Seed B	4	57.1	14.275	0.4825
Seed C	4	64.2	16.05	2.216667

ANOVA

Source of Variation	SS	df	MS	F	P-value	F crit
Rows	12.52917	3	4.176389	6.411514	0.026644	4.757063
Columns	11.25167	2	5.625833	8.636674	0.017135	5.143253
Error	3.908333	6	0.651389			
Total	27.68917	11				

We can test for differences in average plant height across soil plots, where soil plots represents the row variable, as follows:

$H_0: \mu_1 = \mu_2 = \mu_3 = \mu_4$ H_1: At least one of the means differs from the rest.

Decision Rule: For $\alpha = 0.05$ with numerator $df = 3$ and denominator $df = 6$, we will reject the null hypothesis if the calculated test statistic falls above $F = 4.757$.

Test Statistic:

$$F = \frac{MS(Rows)}{MS(Error)} = \frac{4.176389}{0.651389} = 6.412$$

Observed Significance Level:

$$p\text{-value} = 0.0266$$

Conclusion: Since the test statistic of $F = 6.412$ falls above the critical bound of $F = 4.757$, we reject H_0 with at least 95% confidence. Likewise, since the p-value of 0.0266 is less than the desired α of 0.05, we reject H_0. There is enough evidence to conclude that at least one of the soil plots produces different average plant height from the other soil plots.

Answer: Testing Across Seed Varieties

We can test for differences in average plant height across seed varieties, where seed varieties represents the column variable, as follows:

$H_0: \mu_A = \mu_B = \mu_C$ H_1: At least one of the means differs from the rest.

Decision Rule: For $\alpha = 0.05$ with numerator $df = 2$ and denominator $df = 6$, we will reject the null hypothesis if the calculated test statistic falls above $F = 5.143$.

Test Statistic:

$$F = \frac{MS(Columns)}{MS(Error)} = \frac{5.625833}{0.651389} = 8.637$$

Observed Significance Level:

p-value = 0.0171

Conclusion: Since the test statistic of $F = 8.637$ falls above the critical bound of $F = 5.143$, we reject H_0 with at least 95% confidence. Likewise, since the p-value of 0.0171 is less than the desired α of 0.05, we reject H_0. There is enough evidence to conclude that at least one of the seed varieties produces different average plant height from the other seed varieties.

Two-Factor ANOVA With Replication: The Factorial Design With m Observations in Every Cell

Two-factor ANOVA with replication reports the analysis of data captured in a grid with r levels of the row variable, c levels of the column variable, and m data values in every cell of the data grid. The number of replications in the r by c design is m. Two-factor ANOVA with replication allows us to investigate whether the row and column variables are independent of one another or whether the variables interact to affect the values recorded for the dependent variable. This is the comparative benefit of using a factorial design associated with two-factor ANOVA with replication. If interaction effects are not significant, individual row and column effects can be interpreted as they were in the prior section. If an interaction effect exists in the data, the level that occurs on one dimension has some differential effect on the dependent variable depending on the level occurring on the other dimension. For example, if the age and weight class of an athlete have an interactive effect on the time to completion of an athletic event, then a younger and lighter athlete might perform differently than other younger athletes and other lighter athletes.

If interaction effects are significant in the data, individual effects of the row and column variables are difficult to interpret. In the presence of interaction among the row and column variables, we cannot say that the means for the row levels or the means for the column levels are significantly different because the row means change depending on the column level or, alternatively, the column means change depending on the row level. The variables are, in fact, not independent of one another. By removing that variation that is due to interaction, the remaining unexplained variation is reduced, leading to a smaller mean square error and potentially larger, more significant, *F*-ratios for the main effects of the row and column variables than might otherwise be warranted. Finding significant interaction in a set of data complicates our analysis of them, and the researcher should take caution to avoid erroneous interpretations of main effects.

Two-Factor ANOVA With Replication

Interaction effect: H_0: There is no interaction between the row and column variables.

Row variable: H_0: $\mu_1 = \mu_2 = \ldots = \mu_r$

Column variable: H_0: $\mu_1 = \mu_2 = \ldots = \mu_c$

Variations:

$$\text{Total: } SS(\text{Total}) = \sum_{i=1}^{r}\sum_{j=1}^{c}\sum_{k=1}^{m}\left(x_{ijk} - \bar{\bar{x}}\right)^2$$

This is the total fluctuation represented among all data values sampled.

$$\text{Between-Rows Effect: } SS(\text{Row}) = c \cdot m \cdot \sum_{i=1}^{r}\left(\bar{x}_i - \bar{\bar{x}}\right)^2$$

This is the fluctuation between row means and the grand mean weighted by the number of elements within each row. It represents the fluctuation that is *explained* by row identity. Excel output labels the row effect "Sample."

$$\text{Between-Columns Effect: } SS(\text{Column}) = r \cdot m \cdot \sum_{j=1}^{c}\left(\bar{x}_j - \bar{\bar{x}}\right)^2$$

This is the fluctuation between column means and the grand mean weighted by the number of elements within each column. It represents the fluctuation that is *explained* by column identity.

Interaction Effect:
$SS(\text{Interaction}) = SS(\text{Total}) - SS(\text{Row}) - SS(\text{Column}) - SS(\text{Error})$

$$\text{Within-Groups Effect: } SS(\text{Error}) = \sum_{i=1}^{r}\sum_{j=1}^{c}\sum_{k=1}^{m}\left(x_{ijk} - \bar{x}_{ij}\right)^2$$

This is the fluctuation that is *unexplained* by row or column identity. Excel output labels the error effect "Within."

where

$c =$ the number of groups or levels of the independent column variable,

$r =$ the number of groups or levels of the independent row variable,

$m =$ the number of repetitions in the design, or the number of elements sampled in every cell of the data grid,

$\bar{\bar{x}} =$ the grand mean of all elements sampled regardless of what group they are in,

$\bar{x}_j =$ the group mean for elements sampled in column group j,

$\bar{x}_i =$ the group mean for elements sampled in row group i, and

$\bar{x}_{ij} =$ the mean of all values in the cell for the ith row and the jth column.

Example 6.3.

A company's marketing executive ran an experiment on product sales sites. Specifically, she collected product sales completed online, by phone, and in store sites for 4 weeks by weekdays. Since the store and phone sites were closed on Sundays, she limited the data to Mondays through Saturdays. Data are shown in Table 6.4.

Table 6.4. Data for Example 6.3.

	Monday	Tuesday	Wednesday	Thursday	Friday	Saturday
Online	28	25	45	32	46	42
	23	38	40	30	34	48
	13	22	34	32	27	47
	16	29	41	23	30	42
By Phone	17	13	33	32	33	40
	22	12	45	24	34	38
	15	26	36	15	31	38
	5	26	30	13	38	48
In Store	28	29	48	24	40	46
	14	15	42	17	52	45
	27	28	26	23	31	45
	16	24	51	22	35	38

Use a 5% level of significance to analyze mean differences. Specifically test for whether there is any significant interaction between day of week and sales site. If interaction is not significant, test for main effects of day of week and sales site.

Answer: Testing for an Interaction Effect

We can test for an interaction between the two variables day of week and sales site as follows:

H_0: There is no interaction between day of week and sales site.

H_1: There is an interaction between day of week and sales site.

Decision Rule: For $\alpha = 0.05$ with numerator $df = 10$ and denominator $df = 54$, we will reject the null hypothesis if the calculated test statistic falls above $F = 2.011$.

Test Statistic:

$$F = \frac{MS(Interaction)}{MS(Error)} = \frac{25.25833}{44.39352} = 0.569$$

Observed Significance Level:

$$p\text{-value} = 0.8318$$

Conclusion: Since the test statistic of $F = 0.569$ falls below the critical bound of $F = 2.011$, we do not reject H_0 with at least 95% confidence. Likewise, since the p-value of 0.8318 is greater than the desired α of 0.05, we do not reject H_0. There is not enough evidence to conclude that there is any significant interaction between day of week and sales site. Based on this conclusion, we can proceed to test for difference by sales site and by day of week.

Answer: Testing Across Sales Sites

We can test for differences among average sales by sales sites, where sales sites represents the row variable, as follows:

Table 6.5. Two-Factor ANOVA With Replication

SUMMARY	Monday	Tuesday	Wednesday	Thursday	Friday	Saturday	Total
Online							
Count	4	4	4	4	4	4	24
Sum	80	114	160	117	137	179	787
Average	20	28.5	40	29.25	34.25	44.75	32.79167
Variance	46	48.33333	20.66667	18.25	69.58333	10.25	95.91123
By Phone							
Count	4	4	4	4	4	4	24
Sum	59	77	144	84	136	164	664
Average	14.75	19.25	36	21	34	41	27.66667
Variance	50.91667	60.91667	42	76.66667	8.666667	22.66667	133.1884
In Store							
Count	4	4	4	4	4	4	24
Sum	85	96	167	86	158	174	766
Average	21.25	24	41.75	21.5	39.5	43.5	31.91667
Variance	52.91667	40.66667	124.25	9.666667	83	13.66667	141.9928
Total							
Count	12	12	12	12	12	12	
Sum	224	287	471	287	431	517	
Average	18.66667	23.91667	39.25	23.91667	35.91667	43.08333	
Variance	49.51515	56.44697	57.29545	44.08333	50.99242	15.35606	

ANOVA						
Source of Variation	**SS**	**df**	**MS**	**F**	**P-value**	**F crit**
Sample	360.75	2	180.375	4.063093	0.02271	3.168246
Columns	5885.292	5	1177.058	26.51419	2E-13	2.38607
Interaction	252.5833	10	25.25833	0.568964	0.831789	2.011181
Within	2397.25	54	44.39352			
Total	8895.875	71				

$H_0: \mu_{Online} = \mu_{Phone} = \mu_{Store}$ H_1: At least one of the average sales differs by sales site.

Decision Rule: For $\alpha = 0.05$ with numerator $df = 2$ and denominator $df = 54$ we will reject the null hypothesis if the calculated test statistic falls above $F = 3.168$.

Test Statistic:

$$F = \frac{MS(Sample)}{MS(Error)} = \frac{180.375}{44.39352} = 4.063$$

Observed Significance Level:

$$p\text{-value} = 0.0227$$

Conclusion: Since the test statistic of $F = 4.063$ falls above the critical bound of $F = 3.168$, we reject H_0 with at least 95% confidence. Likewise, since the p-value of 0.0227 is less than the desired α of 0.05, we reject H_0. There is enough evidence to conclude that there is a difference in the average sales made at different sales sites.

Answer: Testing Across Days of the Week

We can test for differences among average sales by days of the week, where days of the week represents the column variable, as follows:

$H_0: \mu_M = \mu_{Tu} = \mu_W = \mu_{Th} = \mu_F = \mu_S$ H_1: At least one of the average sales differs by day of week.

Decision Rule: For $\alpha = 0.05$ with numerator $df = 5$ and denominator $df = 54$, we will reject the null hypothesis if the calculated test statistic falls above $F = 2.386$.

Test Statistic:

$$F = \frac{MS(Column)}{MS(Error)} = \frac{1177.058}{44.39352} = 25.514$$

Observed Significance Level:

p-value = 2E-13, which means 2×10^{-13}, which is very small.

Conclusion: Since the test statistic of $F = 25.514$ falls well above the critical bound of $F = 2.386$, we reject H_0 with at least 95% confidence. Likewise, since the p-value of 2×10^{-13} is much smaller than the desired α of 0.05, we reject H_0. There is enough evidence to conclude that there is a difference in the average sales made at different days of the week.

We have shown in Example 6.3. that at least one of the average sales differs by sales site as well as by day of week. There are statistical procedures that can be used to determine which of the pairs of means are significantly different. For example, we can follow up the ANOVA with a test of whether Monday sales differ significantly from Tuesday sales. Care must be taken to properly consider the statistical significance of several pair-wise mean differences taken from the same data set. We will not address the advanced procedures here, but the motivated researcher can access further information using the Tukey simultaneous confidence interval for the difference of two means. The citation can be researched in almost any standard statistical textbook and on the Internet.

CHAPTER 7

Testing Proportions From Two or More Populations

As we have seen in earlier chapters, statistical inference involves a claim about some unknown population characteristic, like the population mean. The techniques used have relied on assumptions about the population the sample data were drawn from. Those techniques are said to be *parametric* in that they measure the degree to which sample data reflect the assumed population *parameter* (for example, μ for a test of population means). In contrast, chi-square (χ^2) analysis examines hypotheses about some property of the distribution being sampled. Chi-square analysis is an example of a set of techniques that are said to be *nonparametric* because they require fewer assumptions about the nature of the population the data were sampled from. In this chapter, we will discuss the chi-square goodness-of-fit test and the test of independence.

Chi-Square Goodness-of-Fit Tests

Chi-square goodness-of-fit tests involve a *multi*nomial distribution—that is, a set of data that represents multiple outcomes within a single population. A multinomial distribution is used to characterize the probabilities that sampled elements fall into their respective classes of a categorical variable. While the goodness-of-fit test can be applied to a population with two outcomes, its strength is shown when applied to a multinomial distribution with three or more outcomes. Consistent with principles set out in our first chapter, multinomial classes must be mutually exclusive and exhaustive. In addition, the probabilities of the multiple outcomes must remain constant trial to trial, and the trials themselves must be independent.

Unlike previous hypothesis tests of population parameters where the null hypothesis contains the opposite of what you really want to be true, the null hypothesis of the chi-square goodness-of-fit test is a constructive statement about the distribution from which the sample could have been taken. In parametric techniques (for the t-, z-, and F-distributions), the alternative hypothesis contains the real motivation for conducting the test. In the goodness-of-fit test, however, the reason for conducting the test is incorporated into the null hypothesis. For the pragmatic analyst conducting a goodness-of-fit test, good news occurs when the null hypothesis cannot be rejected, for the analysis has shown that the sample data do not differ significantly from the distribution specified in the null hypothesis. When the analyst fails to reject the null hypothesis in the goodness-of-fit test, the results present some evidence that the distribution proposed in the null hypothesis can be considered a plausible model for later analysis and forecasting.

The multinomial experiment underlying the goodness-of-fit test requires the sample size to be sufficiently large so that the expected frequencies for each class based on the hypothesized distribution will be at least five. In the event a class has an expected frequency less than five, the analyst should collapse the probability and expected frequency of that class with those of a neighboring class.

Forming hypotheses is the first step of any analytic project. The goodness-of-fit test begins with a hypothesis about the distribution the sample data could have been drawn from.

- H_0: The sample is drawn from a multinomial distribution with specific proportions for each of its classes.
- H_1: The sample is not drawn from a multinomial distribution with specific proportions for each of its classes.

Let's investigate several scenarios.

Scenario 1: According to the 2009 DuPont Global Automotive Color Popularity Report, automotive color rankings worldwide place silver first with 25% of the global market, black second with 23%, white third with 16%, gray fourth with 13%, blue fifth with 9%, and red sixth with 8%. All other car colors make up the remaining 6% of the market. The appropriate null and alternative hypotheses are

- $H_0:$ $p_{Silver} = 0.25, p_{Black} = 0.23, p_{White} = 0.16, p_{Gray} = 0.13,$
  $p_{Blue} = 0.09, p_{Red} = 0.08, p_{Other} = 0.06$

- $H_1:$ At least one of the proportions differs from the stated value.

In this scenario, proportions for each of the possible outcomes are known and add to 1. (Scenario taken from http://www2.dupont.com/Automotive/en_US/news_events/article20091201.html.)

Scenario 2: A county ambulance service provider wants to test whether calls for ambulances are equally distributed over the days of the week. The appropriate null and alternative hypotheses are

- $H_0: p_M = p_{Tu} = p_W = p_{Th} = p_F = p_F = p_{Sat} = p_{Sun} = \dfrac{1}{7}$
- $H_1:$ At least one of the proportions differs from the stated value.

In this scenario, proportions for each of the possible outcomes are assumed to be equal and add to 1.

Scenario 3: A random sample of average grocery expenses for 350 people living in Mannville indicated the sample mean was \$35.34 with a sample standard deviation of \$4.15. Could the sample have been drawn from a normal population with a population mean of \$36 per person? The appropriate null and alternative hypotheses are

- $H_0:$ The sample is from a population of average grocery expenses that are normally distributed around a population mean of \$36.
- $H_1:$ The sample is not from a population of average grocery expenses that are normally distributed around a population mean of \$36.

Note that the distribution in Scenario 3 considers a continuous, quantitative variable. However, by breaking the range of the distribution into segments, we can consider the likelihood that one person's grocery expense falls into any segment and treat the set of expenditure segments as a categorical variable.

In all three scenarios, the null hypothesis contains a constructive statement about the distribution from which the sample could have been taken and against which the sample data will be tested.

The frequency we should expect for each class, E_i, is the expected proportion for each class times the overall sample size, n. Because the null hypothesis is assumed true, the expected values are derived from the null hypothesis. The squared differences between the observed sample frequencies and the expected frequencies are compared to the expected frequencies for each class as a measure of how closely the sample data reflect the hypothesized distribution and form the basis of the test statistic.

χ^2-Test for Goodness-of-Fit

H_0: The sample is drawn from a multinomial distribution with specific proportions for each of its classes.

$$\text{Test Statistic: } \chi^2 = \sum_{i=1}^{k} \frac{\left(O_1 - E_i\right)^2}{E_i}$$

where

O_i are the observed frequencies for each of the i classes,
E_i are the expected frequencies for each of the i classes, and
k is the number of classes being analyzed.

The chi-square distribution is a family of distributions that is highly skewed for small degrees of freedom but approaches the normal distribution for large degrees of freedom.

The degrees of freedom for the chi-square distribution are dependent on the number of population parameters being estimated. In Scenarios 1 and 2, there are no population parameters estimated, so the degrees of freedom in each are simply one less than the number of classes in the multinomial distribution. The degrees of freedom for Scenarios 1 and 2 are $7 - 1 = 6$. In Scenario 3, the null hypothesis specifies the population mean is $36, but it does not specify the value of the population standard deviation. For Scenario 3, the degrees of freedom are one less than the number of classes minus one because we are estimating the population standard deviation. The degrees of freedom for Scenario 3 are $k - 2$, where k is the number of categories in the frequency distribution.

Example 7.1.

Historic performance records for an electronic component indicate that 92% have no evidence of flawed function, 5% show evidence of one flaw, and 3% registered two or more flaws during testing. A sample of 200 components selected from the current batch indicates 179 have no flaws, 12 have one flaw, and 9 have two or more flaws. Is there sufficient reason at the 0.05 level of significance to conclude the current batch has a different performance profile than is historically established?

Answer

$H_0: p_0 = 0.92,$
$p_1 = 0.05,$
$p_{2+} = 0.03$

$H_1:$ At least one proportion differs from the performance profile for this component.

Current performance data mirror the historic performance profile for the component.

At least one of the proportions for performance categories differs from those for the historic performance profile.

Decision Rule: For $df = 3 - 1 = 2$ and $\alpha = 0.05$, we will reject the null hypothesis if the calculated test statistic falls above $\chi^2 = 5.991$. See Table 7.1 below.

Table 7.1. Using the Chi-Square Distribution to Find the Appropriate Critical Bound for df = 2 and α = 0.05

The Chi-Square Distribution: For α = Area in the Upper Tail					
df	0.10	0.05	0.025	0.01	0.005
1	2.706	3.841	5.024	6.635	7.879
2	4.605	5.991	7.378	9.210	10.597
3	6.251	7.815	9.348	11.345	12.838
4	7.779	9.488	11.143	13.277	14.860

Test Statistic:

$$E_1 = 200 \cdot 0.092 = 184, \ E_2 = 200 \cdot 0.05 = 10, \ E_3 = 200 \cdot 0.03 = 6$$

$$\chi^2 = \sum_{i=1}^{3} \frac{\left(O_i - E_i\right)^2}{E_i} = \left(\frac{(179-184)^2}{184} + \frac{(12-10)^2}{10} + \frac{(9-6)^2}{6}\right) = 2.03587$$

Observed Significance Level: Using Excel's built-in function *=chidist* and 2 degrees of freedom, we find that the *p*-value = 0.36134.

Conclusion: Since the test statistic of χ^2 = 2.036 falls below the critical bound of 5.991, we do not reject H_0 with at least 95% confidence. Likewise, since the *p*-value of 0.36 is much greater than the desired α of 0.05, we do not reject H_0. There is not enough evidence to conclude current performance data differ from the historic performance profile for the component. If this were a set of criteria to determine salability, the current batch of components could be shipped to the vendor.

An important application of the goodness-of-fit test is the test for normality. It is a complex procedure, but worthy of developing an example to discuss.

Example 7.2.

According to a regional study, the average weekly grocery expense in an area in 2010 was $36 per person. The results of a random sample of 350 people living in Mannville are shown in Table 7.2. Could the sample have been drawn from a normal population with a population mean of $36 per person? Use a 99% level of confidence.

Answer

Table 7.2. Observed Frequencies for Weekly Grocery Expenses

Weekly Grocery Expenses	Observed Frequencies
$27.50–$29.99	35
$30.00–$32.49	55
$32.50–$34.99	91
$35.00–$37.49	68
$37.50–$39.99	47
$40.00–$42.49	30
$42.50–$44.99	24
Total	350

Some work needs to be done before the formal hypothesis test is conducted. First we need to compute the standard deviation for the sample using the estimation procedures we presented in Chapter 2.

Table 7.3. Computational Table to Support Estimate of Standard Deviation

Bin	Frequency (f_i)	Class Mark (m_i)	$f_i \cdot m_i$	$f_i \cdot m_i^2$
$27.50–$29.99	35	28.75	1006.25	28929.69
$30.00–$32.49	55	31.25	1718.75	53710.94
$32.50–$34.99	91	33.75	3071.25	103654.7
$35.00–$37.49	68	36.25	2465	89356.25
$37.50–$39.99	47	38.75	1821.25	70573.44
$40.00–$42.49	30	41.25	1237.5	51046.88
$42.50–$44.99	24	43.75	1050	45937.5
Total	350		12370	443209.375

$$s^2 = \frac{\sum_{i=1}^{k} f_i m_i^2 - n\bar{x}^2}{n-1} = \frac{443209.4 - 350 \cdot \left(\frac{12370}{350}\right)^2}{349} = 17.2442 \quad s = \sqrt{17.2442} = 4.15$$

We use the calculated standard deviation to compute the z-score that corresponds to each of the bin boundaries, and, from the z-scores, compute the amount of area that occurs under the standard normal curve between subsequent pairs of z-scores. Note that we are using the hypothesized value of the population mean, μ, in the calculation of the z-score, not the sample mean, $\bar{x}$, because the question posed whether the data could have come from a normal population with a mean of $36.

Table 7.4. Computation of z-Scores for Bin Boundaries

Bin	Boundary Score	$z\text{-Score} = \dfrac{x - \mu}{s}$	z-Score
$27.50–$29.99	30.0	$(30 - 36) / 4.15$	-1.44
$30.00–$32.49	32.5	$(32.5 - 36) / 4.15$	-0.84
$32.50–$34.99	35.0	$(35 - 36) / 4.15$	-0.24
$35.00–$37.49	37.5	$(37.5 - 36) / 4.15$	0.36
$37.50–$39.99	40.0	$(40 - 36) / 4.15$	0.96
$40.00–$42.49	42.5	$(42.5 - 36) / 4.15$	1.57
$42.50–$44.99	45.0	$(45 - 36) / 4.15$	2.17

The area in the left tail is simply found on the z-table as the amount of area below a z-score of –1.44. The area of the second region is found by taking the area below a z-score of –0.84, which is 0.2005 and then subtracting the area to the left of its lower bound, which yields 0.1254, and so on, across each region of the distribution.

Once we know the probability of each region, we use those probabilities to compute the expected frequency for each bin by multiplying the probability times the 350 people sampled.

Table 7.5. Computation of Expected Values for Key Regions

Bin	z-Score	Probability	Expected Value
$27.50–$29.99	–$1.44	0.0749	26.215
$30.00–$32.49	–$0.84	0.1256	43.96
$32.50–$34.99	–$0.24	0.2047	71.645
$35.00–$37.49	0.36	0.2354	82.39
$37.50–$39.99	0.96	0.1909	66.815
$40.00–$42.49	1.57	0.1103	38.605
$42.50–$44.99	2.17	0.0432	15.12
$45.00 +		0.015	5.25

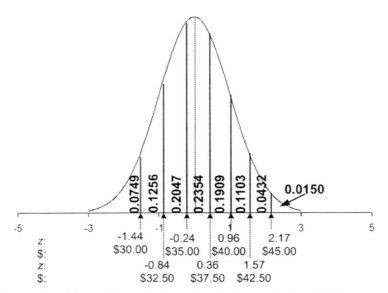

Figure 7.1. Normal Distribution Showing Areas for Key Regions

We are now ready to begin the hypothesis test.

- H_0: The sample is from a population of average grocery expenses that are normally distributed around a population mean of $36.
- H_1: The sample is not from a population of average grocery expenses that are normally distributed around a population mean of $36.

Decision Rule: The null hypothesis contains the assumption that $\mu = 36$, but there is no assumption about the value of the standard deviation. So our degrees of freedom must be reduced by an additional degree. For $df = k - 2 = 8 - 2 = 6$ and $\alpha = 0.01$, the critical bound of the rejection region is $\chi^2 = 16.812$. We will reject the null hypothesis if the test statistic is greater than 16.812.

Test Statistic:

Table 7.6. Computation of Chi-Square Test Statistic

Bin	O_i	E_i	$\chi^2 = \sum_{i=1}^{8} \dfrac{(O_i - E_i)^2}{E_i}$
< 30	35	26.215	2.943971963
32.5	55	43.96	2.77255687
35	91	71.645	5.228781143
37.5	68	82.39	2.513315936
40	47	66.815	5.8764383
42.5	30	38.605	1.918042352
45	24	15.12	5.215238095
> 45	0	5.25	5.25
			Sum = 31.71834466

$$\chi^2 = 31.718$$

Observed Significance Level: Using Excel's built-in function *=chidist* and 6 degrees of freedom, we find the p-value = 1.848×10^{-5}.

Conclusion: Since the test statistic of $\chi^2 = 31.718$ falls above the critical bound of 16.812, we reject H_0 with at least 99% confidence. Likewise, since the p-value of 1.848×10^{-5} is much smaller than the desired α of 0.01, we reject H_0. There is sufficient evidence to conclude that the sample of 350 weekly grocery expenses could not have come from a normal distribution with a mean of $36.

Tests of Independence

The independence of two qualitative variables can be determined using the chi-square test, provided the two variables are each parsed into two or more subcategories. The chi-square test of independence can be used analyzing data involving two categorical variables, where the data are arranged in a grid of *r* rows and *c* columns called a *contingency table*.

By assuming the two variables are independent of one another, we can use the chi-square statistic to measure how much difference there is between actual and expected counts in each of the classes. But how does that work? When two events are independent, the fact that one event occurs does not influence the probability that the other event also occurs. So the joint probability of the two events occurring is the simple probability that one event occurs times the simple probability the other event occurs. In a contingency table, that means that the joint probability a sampled element is in a given row and column equals the simple probability the element is in a given row times the simple probability it is also in that particular column. Each of those simple probabilities is the total number of sampled elements in that row or column divided by the number of elements sampled. Under the assumption of independence between the row variable and the column variable, the following is true:

$$P(row\ i\ and\ column\ j) = P(row\ i) \cdot P(column\ j) = \frac{\Sigma\,(row\ i)}{n} \cdot \frac{\Sigma\,(column\ j)}{n}$$

To compute the chi-square test statistic, we need the expected value. That is the product of the joint probability times the number of elements sampled.

$$E_{(ij)} = P(row\ i\ and\ column\ j) \cdot n = \frac{\Sigma\ (row\ i)}{n} \cdot \frac{\Sigma\ (column\ j)}{n} \cdot n$$

The computational shortcut, then is to cancel one factor of n from the numerator and one from the denominator on the right side of the equation, which means the expected value for each cell is computed by multiplying the sum of elements in that cell's row times the sum of elements in that cell's column divided by the total number of elements sampled.

$$E_{(ij)} = \frac{\Sigma\ (row\ i) \cdot \Sigma\ (column\ j)}{n}$$

χ^2-Test of Independence

H_0: The two categorical variables are independent of each other.

$$\text{Test Statistic: } \chi^2 = \sum_{i=1}^{r} \sum_{j=1}^{c} \frac{\left(O_{ij} - E_{ij}\right)^2}{E_{ij}}$$

where

r = the number of rows in the row variable defined on the left of the contingency table,

c = the number of columns in the column variable defined at the top of the contingency table,

O_{ij} are the observed sample frequencies in each cell, and

E_{ij} are the expected frequencies for each cell, and

$df = (r-1)(c-1)$.

Example 7.3.

The Bureau of Transportation Statistics tracks and reports on-time performance for major commercial airline carriers in the United States. The top seven airline carriers ranked on overall percentage of reported flight operations arriving on time for operations 09/1987 through 10/2010 are shown in Table 7.7.

Table 7.7. U.S. Flight Operations, 9/1987 Through 10/2010

Airline	Rank	Flights On Time (%)	Flights Delayed (%)
Southwest	1	81.9	18.1
Continental	2	78.2	21.8
US Airways	3	78.2	21.8
American	4	78.0	22.0
Delta	5	77.6	22.4
Alaska	6	76.1	23.9
United	7	76.1	23.9

Answer

Assuming samples of 1000 flights per airline, use the 0.05 level of significance to determine whether being on time is independent of individual airlines.

H_0: Being on time is independent H_1: Being on time is dependent of individual airlines.   on individual airlines.

Decision Rule: For $df = (r - 1)(c - 1) = (7 - 1)(2 - 1) = 6$ and $\alpha = 0.05$, we will reject the null hypothesis if the calculated test statistic falls above $\chi^2 = 12.592$.

Test Statistic: For 1000 flights per airline, the observed frequencies are shown in Table 7.8.

Table 7.8. Calculation of the Observed Frequencies per 1000 Flights

Airline	On Time	Delayed	Total
Southwest	819	181	1000
Continental	782	218	1000
US Airways	782	218	1000
American	780	220	1000
Delta	776	224	1000
Alaska	761	239	1000
United	761	239	1000
Sums	**5461**	**1539**	**7000**

To compute the expected values, use Table 7.9.

Table 7.9. Calculation of Expected Values per 1000 Flights

	For On-Time Flights	For Delayed Flights
Southwest	$\dfrac{5467 \cdot 1000}{7000} = 780.14285$	$\dfrac{1539 \cdot 1000}{7000} = 219.857143$
Continental	$\dfrac{5467 \cdot 1000}{7000} = 780.14285$	$\dfrac{1539 \cdot 1000}{7000} = 219.857143$
US Airways	$\dfrac{5467 \cdot 1000}{7000} = 780.14285$	$\dfrac{1539 \cdot 1000}{7000} = 219.857143$
American	$\dfrac{5467 \cdot 1000}{7000} = 780.14285$	$\dfrac{1539 \cdot 1000}{7000} = 219.857143$
Delta	$\dfrac{5467 \cdot 1000}{7000} = 780.14285$	$\dfrac{1539 \cdot 1000}{7000} = 219.857143$
Alaska	$\dfrac{5467 \cdot 1000}{7000} = 780.14285$	$\dfrac{1539 \cdot 1000}{7000} = 219.857143$
United	$\dfrac{5467 \cdot 1000}{7000} = 780.14285$	$\dfrac{1539 \cdot 1000}{7000} = 219.857143$

To review how each cell's contribution to the chi-square test statistic is formed, we include detail of the calculation for Southwest's on-time flights, the first row and the first column of the data:

$$\frac{(O_{1,1} - E_{1,1})^2}{E_{1,1}} = \frac{(819 - 780.142857)^2}{780.142857} = 1.935386 \quad \text{as shown in Table 7.10}$$

The contributions toward the test statistic are shown in Table 7.10.

Table 7.10. Calculation of the Chi-Square Test Statistic

Airline	On Time	Delayed
Southwest	1.935386	6.867539
Continental	0.004421	0.015687
US Airways	0.004421	0.015687
American	2.62E-05	9.28E-05
Delta	0.022	0.078066
Alaska Air	0.46972	1.666759
United	0.46972	1.666759
Sums	**2.905695**	**10.31059**
Grand Total	13.21629	

$$\chi^2 = 13.216$$

Observed Significance Level: Using Excel's built-in function =*chidist* and 6 degrees of freedom, we find the *p*-value = 0.0397.

Conclusion: Since the test statistic of χ^2 = 13.216 falls above the critical bound of 12.592, we reject H_0 with at least 95% confidence. Likewise, since the *p*-value of 0.0397 is less than the desired α of 0.05, we reject H_0. There is enough evidence to conclude that the on-time performance of airline flights is dependent on individual airlines. Said another way, there is evidence to conclude that the percent of on-time flights differs across the top seven major U.S. commercial airlines. (Example taken from http://airconsumer.ost .dot.gov/reports/2010/December/2010DecemberATCR.DOC.)

CHAPTER 8

Analyzing Bivariate Data

We often find it telling to collect data that track two quantitative variables simultaneously. We may want to look at changes in one variable as it changes with or perhaps even influences values of a second variable. How loosely or tightly connected two variables are can be quantified using the methods introduced in this chapter. One method, called regression analysis, explores whether we can improve our estimate of one variable by knowing the value of the other variable for an element of the population being studied. A unique benefit of regression analysis arises from the regression model itself: We can use the regression model to predict values of interest from information that is already known. By using recent information on automobile loan rates, for example, we can anticipate the rate we might qualify for as we decide what car to buy. Knowing how the rates have changed over time in recent weeks or even days, we can better predict the rate we can lock in at the time of our purchase. By knowing sales of a product in recent days, managers can better estimate how deep an inventory to maintain and how often to refresh their order to meet but not greatly exceed consumer demand for the product. Or, by knowing the annual return on a stock, a trader might be able to predict its future market value. Values of interest are sometimes dependent on several inputs. The market value of a stock, for example, may be influenced by a number of factors. We will limit regression analysis in this chapter to the relationship between a single independent variable, x, and its dependent variable, y.

Scatterplots

Sometimes a relationship between two numerical random variables becomes apparent by collecting a random sample of measurements of both variables and looking at an x-y scatterplot of the data. Seldom do we see a relationship between two variables so tightly connected that the scatterplot maps to a straight line. More likely, the data points are somewhat dispersed, or scattered, around the grid. A cloud of data points that generally rises from left to right provides evidence of a *positive* or *direct* relationship between the two variables, whereas a cloud of points that falls from left to right provides evidence of a *negative* or *inverse* relationship between *x*, the independent variable, and *y*, the dependent variable. A cloud of points that appears as a smattering of points with no direction to them provides evidence that the value of *y* is unrelated to the value of *x*.

An important note is appropriate here. Undoubtedly, in your first-year algebra course years ago, you were told the *x*-axis represented the independent variable and the *y*-axis the dependent variable. Although the definitions have been with us for years, it was probably a moment of dazzling insight when you first realized that one variable in your business setting might be changing with another, may even be causing changes in another variable. In fact, scatterplots are most compelling when the independent variable is cast as the cause and the dependent variable as its effect. Echoes of the dependent variable as a *function of x* take on new meaning when depicted in an *x-y*, an *independent-dependent*, a *cause-effect* scatterplot. While the primary goal of this text is an improved understanding of statistics, we must not lose sight of the fact that the powerful notion that one element in your business setting causes changes in another is a constructive insight born from extensive experience.

Example 8.1.

Is there a relationship between the annual average 6-month Treasury Bill rates and the inflation rate based on the Consumer Price Index (CPI) for urban Americans? To develop a preliminary sense of an answer, we gathered the 27 observations from 1982 through 2008, as shown in Table 8.1.

Comment on whether there seems to be a relationship between the annual average 6-month Treasure Bill rates and inflation as based on the CPI. If we knew nothing about the average 6-month Treasury Bill rates, what would we guess the average inflation rate

Table 8.1. Annual Average 6-Month Treasury Bill Rates With Annual Inflation Based on the Consumer Price Index (CPI)

	Avg 6-Mo T-Bill Rate	CPI Inflation		Avg 6-Mo T-Bill Rate	CPI Inflation
1982	11.06	6.09	1995	5.56	2.9
1983	8.74	3.19	1996	5.08	2.82
1984	9.78	4.37	1997	5.18	2.41
1985	7.65	3.56	1998	4.83	1.63
1986	6.02	1.64	1999	4.75	2.17
1987	6.03	3.75	2000	5.90	3.27
1988	6.91	4.02	2001	3.34	2.83
1989	8.03	4.83	2002	1.68	1.62
1990	7.46	5.35	2003	1.05	2.39
1991	5.44	4.36	2004	1.58	2.65
1992	3.54	2.95	2005	3.39	3.32
1993	3.12	3.03	2006	4.81	3.23
1994	4.64	2.52	2007	4.44	2.9
			2008	1.62	3.78

to be? If we knew the annual average 6-month Treasury Bill rate was 10%, what would we guess the inflation rate to be?

Answer

In this problem, the annual average 6-month Treasury Bill rate is being used to predict the rate of inflation based on the CPI. So the annual average 6-month Treasury Bill rate is the independent variable on the x-axis, and the rate of inflation based on the CPI is the dependent variable on the y-axis.

Interpretation: The data cloud in Figure 8.1 seems to be rising left to right, indicating there is a positive, or direct, relationship between the annual average 6-month Treasury Bill rate and the annual rate of inflation as based on the CPI.

If we knew nothing about the average 6-month Treasury Bill rate, we would guess the average inflation rate to be a little over 3%. But if we knew the annual average 6-month Treasury Bill rate was 10%, we would guess the annual rate of inflation to be around 4.5%.

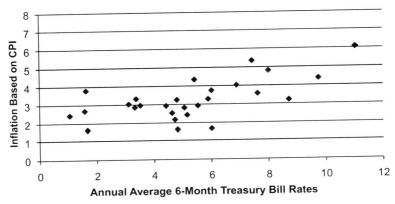

Figure 8.1. Scatterplot of the Annual Average 6-Month Treasury Bill Rates With Annual Inflation Based on the Consumer Price Index (CPI)

The Least Squares Linear Regression Equation

The direction and location of the cloud of points and the width of the point cloud depicted in the scatterplot are all important characteristics of the relationship between the independent variable, x, and the dependent variable, y. Later in this chapter we will investigate the width, or spread, of the points around the grid. First we need a more precise way to establish the direction and location of the point cloud.

While the best model of the x-y relationship depends on the distribution of the variables seen in the scatterplot, the simplest model for a set of two-dimensional data points is a straight line. Recall from algebra that the equation for a straight line depends on the slope, m, and the y-intercept, b, and is given by the equation

$$y = mx + b$$

This is the *slope-intercept form* of the equation, where the intercept, b, is a fixed, constant value and the slope, m or rise over run, captures the variable component of the relationship between x and y.

In statistics, we report the intercept constant first followed by the variable component. To predict an individual value of y_i, we use the following equation:

> ### The Least Squares Linear Regression Equation
>
> $$\hat{y}_i = b_0 + b_1 x_i$$
>
> where
>
> b_0 is the constant value of the y-intercept,
> b_1 is the slope of the line through the point cloud, and
> x_i is the value of the independent variable for which we want to
>   estimate the value of the dependent variable.

There are many lines that can flow through a cloud of points, so we need a criterion for selecting a specific straight line. The criterion used in simple linear regression is to minimize the squared differences between the actual y-value and the predicted y-value for any given value of x. Hence this line is called the *least squares regression line*. In this equation, the intercept is b_0, which establishes the location of the point cloud along the y-axis when x has a value of zero, and the slope is b_1, which captures the direction of the point cloud. The subscript "i" denotes that there is a specific x-value along the x-axis for which we want to predict a related y-value, $\hat{y}$.

In fact, the values reflected in the regression equation can be seen as the sample estimates of their respective population parameters. The value of $\hat{y}_i$ is the estimate based on sample data for the actual values of y_i. The values for b_0 and b_1 are based on the random sample estimating the true population parameters β_0 and β_1, respectively.

Example 8.2.

Use Excel to develop the least squares regression line that uses the annual average 6-month Treasury Bill rates shown in Table 8.1 to predict the inflation rate based on the CPI for urban Americans. If we knew the annual average 6-month Treasury Bill rate was 10%, using the regression line, what would we guess the inflation rate to be?

Answer

Using Excel's Data Analysis toolkit, the regression analysis for the data produced the output shown in Table 8.1.

Table 8.2. Regression Analysis

SUMMARY OUTPUT

Regression Statistics	
Multiple R	0.63769154
R Square	0.40665051
Adjusted R Square	0.38291653
Standard Error	0.85511732
Observations	27

ANOVA

	df	SS	MS	F	Significance F
Regression	1	12.52858879	12.5285888	17.1336838	0.0003462
Residual	25	18.28064084	0.73122563		
Total	26	30.80922963			

	Coefficients	Standard Error	t Stat	p-value	Lower 95%	Upper 95%
Intercept	1.78773235	0.388338389	4.60354268	0.00010413	0.987935	2.58753
Annual Avg 6-Mo T-Bill	0.27756285	0.067055741	4.13928542	0.0003462	0.1394591	0.41567

The regression coefficient for the y-intercept, b_0, is 1.7877 and the regression coefficient for the slope, b_1, is 0.2776. The least squares regression line is given as $\hat{y}_i = 1.7877 + 0.2776x_i$. For $x = 10$, we would predict the inflation rate to be $\hat{y}_i = 1.7877 + 0.2776 \cdot 10 = 4.5634$. So, when the annual average Treasury Bill rate is 10%, we would predict the inflation rate to be 4.56%. Note, some differences due to rounding may occur.

Interpretation: The slope of the regression line captures the direction of the point cloud, showing y generally increases 0.2776% for each percent increase in the annual average 6-month Treasury Bill rate. The y-intercept of 1.7877 anchors the regression line at the point (0, 1.7877) and provides the reference point, the beginning of the change captured in the slope, for the location of the point cloud on the y-axis.

To add the regression line to the scatterplot, we simply right-click the mouse on any data point in the plot, click "Add Trendline," select "Linear," and indicate that the equation should be shown on the graph. Notice that the linear trendline is the regression line.

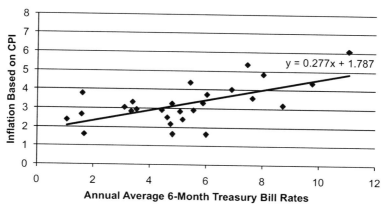

Figure 8.2. Annual Average 6-Month Treasury Bill Rates With Annual Inflation Based on the Consumer Price Index (CPI) With Linear Trendline

The Assumptions of Regression

We have learned to estimate the slope and the y-intercept of the line that best fits the point cloud exhibited by a set of two-dimensional data. If the data points were perfectly predicted by the regression line, all of the points would fall right on that line. But fluctuation is the rule not the exception in sets of real data. The width of the point cloud around the regression line is also an important characteristic to assess in our analysis of the regression model. In general, the more dispersed the point cloud is around the regression line, the less powerful the regression model is in predicting the actual y-values. Conversely, the more narrowly the point cloud aligns around the regression line, the more powerful the regression model is in predicting the y-values.

Four major assumptions underlie the model of simple linear regression:

1. The nature of the relationship between x and y is linear.
2. The errors in y—that is, the differences between the actual value for y and the value for y predicted by the regression line $(y_i - \hat{y}_i)$—are normally distributed around the regression line for any given value of x_i.
3. The distribution of the errors, those differences between the actual value for y and the value for y predicted by the regression line, $(y_i - \hat{y}_i)$, around the regression line is constant regardless of the value of x.
4. The values of $(y_i - \hat{y}_i)$ are independent of one another and of any given value of x_i.

The errors in estimating each y based on the value of each x are called *residuals*.

The normal distribution of the errors, or residuals, at any point along the regression line is the same as the normal distribution of the errors at every other point along the regression line. It is as if a single unchanging normal distribution slides along the regression line to generate the errors. The standard deviation of the estimate, s_e, is an estimate based on sample data of the standard deviation of the normal distribution of errors.

Figure 8.3 contains the calculations for $(y_i - \hat{y}_i)$, the differences between the actual value for y and the value for y predicted by the

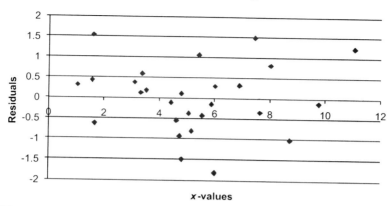

Figure 8.3. Scatterplot of the Residuals in y Against the x-Values

regression line, where $\hat{y}_i = 1.7877 + 0.2776x_i$ was used to generate the scatterplot in Figure 8.2.

From the values shown in Table 8.3, we form the scatterplot of resulting residuals against the independent variable shown in Figure 8.3. The pattern in Figure 8.3 trends downward for increasing values of the independent variable. Ideally, we would like to see no pattern of increasing or decreasing residuals in the scatterplot. But the regression analysis results are still useful in providing a test of whether there is a relationship between the annual average 6-month Treasury Bill rate and the CPI inflation, and for making improved estimates of CPI inflation based on the value of the annual average 6-month Treasury Bill rate. The scatterplot suggests that the relationship between the annual average 6-month Treasury Bill rate and the CPI inflation may not be a linear relationship. Advanced regression techniques can be used to look at nonlinear models.

The Standard Error of the Estimate

The degree to which the *y*-values fluctuate around the regression line affects the explanatory power of the analysis. The standard error of the estimate, s_e, is a measure of error generated by using the regression equation, $\hat{y}$, to predict the actual values of *y*. Specifically, if the residuals are assumed to

Table 8.3. Original Data for x and y, Augmented by Predicted y-Values, Residuals, and Squared Residuals

	Avg 6-Mo T-Bill Rate	CPI Inflation	y-Hat	Residuals	Squared Residuals
1982	11.06	6.09	4.857577	1.23242252	1.518865267
1983	8.74	3.19	4.213632	-1.023631666	1.047821788
1984	9.78	4.37	4.502297	-0.132297031	0.017502504
1985	7.65	3.56	3.911088	-0.351088159	0.123262895
1986	6.02	1.64	3.458661	-1.818660712	3.307526784
1987	6.03	3.75	3.461436	0.28856366	0.083268986
1988	6.91	4.02	3.705692	0.314308351	0.09878974
1989	8.03	4.83	4.016562	0.813437958	0.661681312
1990	7.46	5.35	3.858351	1.491648783	2.225016092
1991	5.44	4.36	3.297674	1.062325742	1.128535982
1992	3.54	2.95	2.770305	0.179695159	0.03229035
1993	3.12	3.03	2.653728	0.376271556	0.141580284
1994	4.64	2.52	3.075624	-0.555623977	0.308718004
1995	5.56	2.9	3.330982	-0.4309818	0.185745312
1996	5.08	2.82	3.197752	-0.377751632	0.142696295
1997	5.18	2.41	3.225508	-0.815507917	0.665053162
1998	4.83	1.63	3.128361	-1.498360919	2.245085444
1999	4.75	2.17	3.106156	-0.936155891	0.876387852
2000	5.90	3.27	3.425353	-0.155353169	0.024134607
2001	3.34	2.83	2.714792	0.115207729	0.013272821
2002	1.68	1.62	2.254038	-0.634037939	0.402004108
2003	1.05	2.39	2.079173	0.310826657	0.096613211
2004	1.58	2.65	2.226282	0.423718346	0.179537237
2005	3.39	3.32	2.72867	0.591329586	0.34967068
2006	4.81	3.23	3.12281	0.107190338	0.011489769
2007	4.44	2.9	3.020111	-0.120111407	0.01442675
2008	1.62	3.78	2.237384	1.542615832	2.379663606
				Sum = 18.28064084	

be normally distributed, the standard error of the estimate is the standard deviation of those residuals based on the sample data. The further the actual values of *y* are away from the values of *y* predicted by the regression equation, the larger is the value of the standard error, s_e. The sum of squared residuals is the core of the error term. The sum of squared residuals divided by the degrees of freedom on error generates the value of SSE, summed squared error, which we find on the Excel printout.

Standard Error of the Estimate, s_e

$$s_e = \sqrt{\frac{(y_i - \hat{y}_i)^2}{n - 2}} = \sqrt{\frac{SSE}{n - 2}} = \sqrt{MSE}$$

where

s_e = the standard error of the estimate for $\hat{y}$,
y_i = the actual y-value for each data point,
$\hat{y}_i$ = the predicted y-value for each data point,
SSE = the error sum of squares,
MSE = the error mean square, and
n = the number of data points in the sample.

This is the same SSE that we discussed in Chapter 6. The degrees of freedom in simple linear regression are the number of data points minus 2, $(n - 2)$. The ratio of SSE divided by $(n - 2)$ is MSE, and the square root of MSE is called the standard error of the estimate for $\hat{y}$, or s_e. In terms of our analysis,

$$s_e = \sqrt{\frac{(y_i - \hat{y}_i)^2}{n - 2}} = \sqrt{MSE}$$

$$= \sqrt{\frac{18.2806}{27 - 2}} = \sqrt{0.7312} = 0.8551$$

The reader can verify the values on the Excel printout contained in Example 8.2.

Using the Regression Model for Estimation

Regression models are useful not only because they provide evidence about the nature and strength of the relationship between two variables. Regression models are also useful because we can use them to make estimates. With the regression model, we can make three kinds of estimates:

1. Individual point estimates of y for a given value of x
2. Interval estimates for the average value of y for all elements of the population that have a given value of the x-variable
3. Interval estimates for an individual value of y for any single element of the population that has a given value of the x-variable

Caution should be used when making any of these estimates with the regression model, however. The model is most accurate for values of x that are close to $\bar{x}$, the mean x-value. The farther the point of estimation is away from the mean value of x, the less precise is the estimate for the mean of y. Particular caution should be used in pressing a regression model to predict values outside the interval of x-values represented in the observed data.

Point Estimates

Recall that a point estimate is found by substituting the particular value of x into the fitted regression equation to obtain $\hat{y}_i$, the estimated value of y based on the particular value of x_i. Point estimates are easily computed by calculator or on Excel. The point estimate remains important in all predictions, since it is also the center value of both interval estimates.

Confidence Interval Estimates for the Mean of y

The confidence interval estimate for the mean value of y is used to predict the average or expected value of y for a given value of $x = x^*$.

Confidence Interval Estimate for the Mean of y

$$\hat{y} \pm t \cdot s_e \cdot \sqrt{\frac{1}{n} + \frac{(x^* - \bar{x})^2}{\sum (x_i - \bar{x})^2}}$$

where

x^* = the x-value of interest,
$\hat{y}_i$ = the predicted y-value for each data point,
s_e = the standard error of the estimate for $\hat{y}$,
$\bar{x}$ = the average value of x, and
n = the number of data points in the sample.
t = critical bound from t-distribution for desired α and $df = n - 2$

Example 8.3.

Construct and interpret the 95% confidence interval for the mean inflation rate based on the CPI when the annual average 6-month Treasury Bill rate is 6%.

Answer

We need to accrue all the pieces of information necessary to compute the confidence interval.

$$\hat{y}_i = 1.7877 + 0.2776x_i = 1.7877 + 0.2776 \cdot 6 = 3.453$$

t-coefficient for 95% confidence and $df = 25 = 2.060$

$$s_e = 0.8551$$

$$\bar{x} = 5.25$$

$$\sum_{i=1}^{27}(x_i - \bar{x})^2 = 162.6226 \text{ (shown in Table 8.4)}$$

$$\hat{y} \pm t \cdot s_e \cdot \sqrt{\frac{1}{n} + \frac{(x^* - \bar{x})^2}{\sum(x_i - \bar{x})^2}} = 3.453 \pm 2.060 \cdot 0.8551 \cdot \sqrt{\frac{1}{27} + \frac{(6 - 5.25)^2}{162.6226}}$$

$$= 3.453 \pm 0.354$$

Table 8.4. Computation of $\sum_{i=1}^{27}(x_i - \bar{x})^2$

	x	(x – x-bar)²		x	(x – x-bar)²
1982	11.06	33.7561	1996	5.08	0.0289
1983	8.74	12.1801	1997	5.18	0.0049
1984	9.78	20.5209	1998	4.83	0.1764
1985	7.65	5.76	1999	4.75	0.25
1986	6.02	0.5929	2000	5.90	0.4225
1987	6.03	0.6084	2001	3.34	3.6481
1988	6.91	2.7556	2002	1.68	12.7449
1989	8.03	7.7284	2003	1.05	17.64
1990	7.46	4.8841	2004	1.58	13.4689
1991	5.44	0.0361	2005	3.39	3.4596
1992	3.54	2.9241	2006	4.81	0.1936
1993	3.12	4.5369	2007	4.44	0.6561
1994	4.64	0.3721	2008	1.62	13.1769
1995	5.56	0.0961		Sum = 162.6226	

$$\text{Lower bound} = 3.453 - 0.354 = 3.099$$

$$\text{Upper bound} = 3.453 + 0.354 = 3.807$$

Interpretation: Over all years in which the annual average 6-month Treasury Bill rate is 6%, the mean inflation rate based on the CPI will fall between 3.099% and 3.807% with 95% confidence.

Prediction Interval Estimates for Individual Values of y

The prediction interval estimate for the individual value of y is used to predict the particular value of y for a given value of $x = x^*$.

Prediction Interval Estimate for an Individual Value of y

$$\hat{y} \pm t \cdot s_e \cdot \sqrt{1 + \frac{1}{n} + \frac{\left(x^* - \bar{x}\right)^2}{\sum\left(x_i - \bar{x}\right)^2}}$$

where

x^* = the x-value of interest,

$\hat{y}_i$ = the predicted y-value for each data point,

s_e = the standard error of the estimate for $\hat{y}$,

$\bar{x}$ = the average value of x, and

n = the number of data points in the sample.

t = critical bound from t-distribution for desired α and $df = n - 2$

Example 8.4.

Construct and interpret the 95% prediction interval for an inflation rate based on the CPI when the annual average 6-month Treasury Bill rate is 6%.

Answer

Using the same information provided in Example 8.3,

$$\hat{y} \pm t \cdot s_e \cdot \sqrt{1 + \frac{1}{n} + \frac{\left(x^* - \bar{x}\right)^2}{\sum\left(x_i - \bar{x}\right)^2}} = 3.453 \pm 2.060 \cdot 0.8551 \cdot \sqrt{1 + \frac{1}{27} + \frac{(6 - 5.25)^2}{162.6226}}$$

$$= 3.453 \pm 1.796$$

Lower bound = 3.453 − 1.796 = 1.657

Upper bound = 3.453 + 1.796 = 5.249

Interpretation: For an individual year in which the annual average 6-month Treasury Bill rate is 6%, the inflation rate based on the CPI will fall between 1.657% and 5.249% with 95% confidence.

Suppose we had only collected the sample data for CPI inflation (but not for the average 6-month Treasury Bill rate) and wanted to find an interval estimate for the CPI inflation rate next year based on the annual CPI inflation rates between 1982 and 2008. Using the methods from Chapter 3, the point estimate would have been 3.2437% and an interval estimate with a 95% confidence level would have been between 1.006% and 5.481%, using the following calculations:

$$\bar{x} \pm t \cdot s = 3.2437 \pm 2.056 \cdot 1.089 = 3.2437 \pm 2.2390$$

Comparing this to the prior interval from Example 8.4, we see the regression model creates a narrower, more precise interval estimate for the same level of confidence, along with adjusting the center of the interval estimate based on the association with the 6-month Treasury Bill rate.

Coefficients of Determination and Correlation

While the width of the point cloud around its regression line gives us an insight into how consistent the regression model is in predicting the actual y-values, we do not yet have a method to measure how powerful that relationship is between x and y.

The Coefficient of Determination

An important measure of the strength of the linear relationship between x and y is the percent of the total variation in y that is explained by the variation in x. It is the *coefficient of determination*, r^2. Taking advantage of earlier calculations, we define the explained variation in y as the complement of the unexplained variation, or sum of squared residuals.

The Coefficient of Determination, r^2

$$r^2 = 1 - \frac{\sum(y_i - \hat{y}_i)^2}{\sum(y_i - \bar{y})^2} = 1 - \frac{SSE}{SSTotal} = \frac{SSR}{SSTotal}$$

where

y_i = the actual y-value for each data point;

$\hat{y}_i$ = the predicted y-value for each data point;

$\bar{y}$ = the average y-value,

$\sum(y_i - \hat{y}_i)$ = SSE = the error sum of squares, the variation in y that is *not* explained by the regression model; and

$\sum(y_i - \bar{y})^2$ = $SSTotal$ = the total sum of squares, the total variation in y-values,

SSR = the regression sum of squares, the variation in y that is explained by the regression model.

Example 8.5.

Calculate and interpret the coefficient of determination for the regression of the inflation CPI on the annual average 6-month Treasury Bill rates.

Answer

The coefficient of determination is calculated as follows:

$$r^2 = 1 - \frac{\sum(y_i - \hat{y}_i)^2}{\sum(y_i - \bar{y})^2} = 1 - \frac{SSE}{SSTotal} = \frac{SSR}{SSTotal}$$

$$= 1 - \frac{18.2806}{30.8092} = \frac{12.5286}{30.8092} = 0.40665$$

The reader can confirm the value for R Square in the Excel output under "Regression Statistics."

Interpretation: Nearly 40.7% of the total fluctuation in the inflation rate based on the CPI is explained by changes in the annual average 6-month Treasury Bill rates.

The Coefficient of Correlation

Like the coefficient of determination, the *coefficient of correlation, r,* is also an important measure of the strength of the linear relationship between x and y. But, in addition to serving as a measure of the strength of the regression model, the coefficient of correlation also reflects the direction of the linear relationship between x and y. It addresses the question: do the annual average 6-month Treasury Bill rates and the rates of inflation based on the CPI increase or decrease in a related way? The coefficient of correlation is related to the coefficient of determination: specifically, the value of the coefficient of correlation is r, the square root of the coefficient of determination, and has the same sign as the slope of the regression model. In terms of the particular data we have been analyzing, the sign of r is positive because the regression slope is positive ($b_1 = +0.2776$). The value of r is given by the square root of 0.40665, or 0.63769, which the reader can verify is the value for Multiple R in the Excel output under "Regression Statistics." If the b1 coefficient in the regression equation had been negative, the coefficient of correlation would have been –0.63769.

Hypothesis Tests for Model Utility

We now have estimates for three of the characteristics important to the linear relationship between the independent variable, x, and the dependent variable, y:

- The y-intercept for the cloud of points, b_0, which estimates β_0
- The direction of the cloud of points, b_1, which estimates β_1, the slope of the regression model, and
- The width of the cloud of points, s_e

We also know how to fit a line through a point cloud using the least squares method. In general, the denser the data points are around the regression line and the steeper the slope of the slope coefficient b_1, the better the regression model is in estimating the value of y. The more dispersed the data points are away from the regression line and the flatter the regression line, the poorer the regression model is in estimating the value of y. We know from the coefficient of determination the percent of total variation in y that is explained by the regression model. What we do not have yet, however, is a tool to tell us how good our regression model is. How close do the data points have to gather around the regression line for us to conclude that our model is doing a better job than simply estimating the value of y based on sample data for the y-variable alone? What amount of confidence can we have in such a conclusion? These are important questions to which we now turn our attention.

The Global F-Test of Model Utility

A test of model utility, or the overall usefulness of the regression model, can be conducted with an F-test. This test answers the question: can we do a better job of predicting actual y-values using the regression model $y = \hat{y}$ than we can by using $y = \bar{y}$, the average value of y? If the value of y does not depend linearly on the value of x, then the regression line provides an estimate for individual values of y that is no better an approximation of y than the average y-value. Stated alternately, if the value of y does not depend linearly on the value of x, then the regression line, $y = \hat{y}$, is virtually the same as the line $y = \bar{y}$. If the regression model is useful, the amount of variance explained by the regression model will be significantly greater than the amount of unexplained variance. Recall from Chapter 6 that the F-statistic is formed by the ratio of two variances, variance that is explained by the variable of interest divided by the unexplained variance. In regression, the F-statistic is formed by the ratio of the mean square regression divided by the mean square error.

Global F-Test for H_0

The regression equation $y = \hat{y}$ does not provide a better prediction for the actual y-values than using $y = \bar{y}$, the average value of y.

$$\textbf{The Test Statistic: } F = \frac{MSR}{MSE} = \frac{SSR/1}{SSE/(n-2)}$$

where

MSR = the regression mean square,

MSE = the error mean square,

SSR = the regression sum of squares, the variation in y that is explained by the regression model.

SSE = the error sum of squares, the variation in y that is *not* explained by the regression model,

n = the number of data points included in the sample, and

df on the F statistic are 1 and $(n-2)$.

Example 8.6.

Looking back on the data from Examples 8.1–8.5, use the global F-test to evaluate whether the regression model $y = \hat{y}$ is a better predictor of the rate of inflation based on the CPI than the horizontal line $y = \bar{y}$. Use $\alpha = 0.05$.

Answer

H_0: The regression equation $y = \hat{y}$ is not useful in predicting the actual values for the inflation rates based on the CPI.

H_1: The regression equation $y = \hat{y}$ is useful in predicting the actual values for the inflation rates based on the CPI.

Decision Rule: For $\alpha = 0.05$ with 1 and $(27 - 2) = 25$ degrees of freedom for the numerator and denominator respectively, we will reject the null hypothesis if the calculated test statistic falls above $F = 4.24$.

Test Statistic:

$$F = \frac{MSR}{MSE} = \frac{12.5286}{0.7312} = 17.1337$$

Observed Significance Level: To find an exact p-value for a t statistic, we use Excel's imbedded function $=Fdist(17.1337,1,25)$, which yields the answer p-value = 0.0003.

Conclusion: Since the test statistic of $F = 17.1337$ falls above the critical bound of $F = 4.24$, we reject H_0 with at least 95% confidence.

Likewise, since the p-value of 0.0003 is less than the desired α of 0.05, we reject H_0. There is enough evidence to conclude that the regression equation does a better job of predicting the actual inflation rates based on the CPI than using the average inflation rate. The average annual 6-month Treasury Bill rates are useful in predicting the CPI inflation rates.

The t-Test for the Slope of the Regression Line

In Example 8.1, we estimated the value of y as if we didn't know anything about the value of x. To do that, we used the average y-value, or $\bar{y}$. In fact, this is the basis for the t-test of how well a regression model fits sample data. In simple linear regression, the t-test is a mirror image of the F-test. Since the line $y = \bar{y}$ has a slope $m = 0$, we can also test the model utility by testing whether the slope of the regression model, β_1, is significantly different from zero. If we are able to reject the null hypothesis, $\beta_1 = 0$, then we have evidence that the regression model, $y = \hat{y}$, is doing a better job of predicting actual values of y than the line $y = \bar{y}$.

---

t-Test for H_0: $\beta_1 = 0$

$$\textbf{The Test Statistic: } t = \frac{b_1}{s_{b_1}}$$

where

β_1 = the slope of the population regression line,
b_1 = the slope of the regression line based on the sample,
s_{b_1} = the standard error of the slope, b_1, and
$df = (n - 2)$ on the t-coefficient.

Example 8.7.

Looking back on the data from Examples 8.1–8.5, use the t-test to evaluate whether the regression model $y = \hat{y}$ is a better predictor of the rate of inflation based on the CPI than the horizontal line $y = \bar{y}$. Use $\alpha = 0.05$.

Answer

$H_0: \beta_1 = 0$

The slope of the population regression line is equal to zero.

$H_1: \beta_1 \neq 0$

The slope of the population regression line is not equal to zero.

Decision Rule: For $\alpha = 0.05$ with $(27 - 2) = 25$ degrees of freedom, we will reject the null hypothesis if the calculated test statistic falls above $t = 2.060$ or below $t = -2.060$.

Test Statistic:

$$t = \frac{b_1}{s_{b_1}} = \frac{0.27756}{0.067056} = 4.139$$

Observed Significance Level: To find an exact p-value for a t statistic, we use Excel's imbedded function $=tdist(4.139,25,2)$, which yields the answer p-value $= 0.0003$.

Conclusion: Since the test statistic of $t = 4.139$ falls above the critical bound of 2.060, we reject H_0 with at least 95% confidence. Likewise, since the p-value of 0.0003 is less than the desired α of 0.05, we reject H_0. There is enough evidence to conclude that the regression equation does a better job of predicting the actual inflation rates based on the CPI than using the average inflation rate. The average annual 6-month Treasury Bill rates are useful in predicting the CPI inflation rates.

Comparing the Global F-Test and the t-Test of Model Utility

It is a reasonable question to ask: what is the relationship between the global F-test and the t-test of the regression coefficient just completed? In simple linear regression, the two tests mirror one another. Notice that the p-value on the t-test is the same as the p-value on the F-test. Both p-values are reported as 0.003462. In fact, the square of the t test statistic, 4.139, equals the F test statistic, 17.1337. The square of the t critical bound, 2.060 or more precisely 2.0595, is the F critical bound, 4.24 or more precisely 4.2417. Both values were rounded and reported here as 2.060 and 4.24. In multiple regression, where more than one independent variable is included in the analysis, the t-test of individual regression coefficients and the global F-test part ways and serve separate purposes. Multiple regression models are not covered in this text.

Appendix

Standard Normal Table (z)

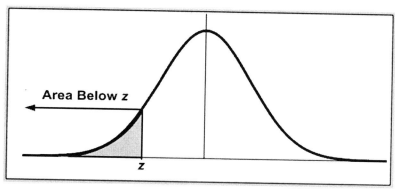

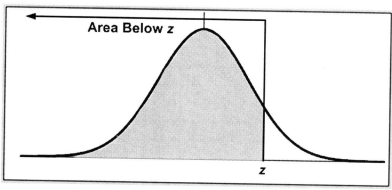

z	.00	.01	.02	.03	.04	.05	.06	.07	.08	.09
-3.8	.0001	.0001	.0001	.0001	.0001	.0001	.0001	.0001	.0001	.0001
-3.7	.0001	.0001	.0001	.0001	.0001	.0001	.0001	.0001	.0001	.0001
-3.6	.0002	.0002	.0001	.0001	.0001	.0001	.0001	.0001	.0001	.0001
-3.5	.0002	.0002	.0002	.0002	.0002	.0002	.0002	.0002	.0002	.0002
-3.4	.0003	.0003	.0003	.0003	.0003	.0003	.0003	.0003	.0003	.0002
-3.3	.0005	.0005	.0005	.0004	.0004	.0004	.0004	.0004	.0004	.0003
-3.2	.0007	.0007	.0006	.0006	.0006	.0006	.0006	.0005	.0005	.0005

z	.00	.01	.02	.03	.04	.05	.06	.07	.08	.09
-3.1	.0010	.0009	.0009	.0009	.0008	.0008	.0008	.0008	.0007	.0007
-3.0	.0013	.0013	.0013	.0012	.0012	.0011	.0011	.0011	.0010	.0010
-2.9	.0019	.0018	.0018	.0017	.0016	.0016	.0015	.0015	.0014	.0014
-2.8	.0026	.0025	.0024	.0023	.0023	.0022	.0021	.0021	.0020	.0019
-2.7	.0035	.0034	.0033	.0032	.0031	.0030	.0029	.0028	.0027	.0026
-2.6	.0047	.0045	.0044	.0043	.0041	.0040	.0039	.0038	.0037	.0036
-2.5	.0062	.0060	.0059	.0057	.0055	.0054	.0052	.0051	.0049	.0048
-2.4	.0082	.0080	.0078	.0075	.0073	.0071	.0069	.0068	.0066	.0064
-2.3	.0107	.0104	.0102	.0099	.0096	.0094	.0091	.0089	.0087	.0084
-2.2	.0139	.0136	.0132	.0129	.0125	.0122	.0119	.0116	.0113	.0110
-2.1	.0179	.0174	.0170	.0166	.0162	.0158	.0154	.0150	.0146	.0143
-2.0	.0228	.0222	.0217	.0212	.0207	.0202	.0197	.0192	.0188	.0183
-1.9	.0287	.0281	.0274	.0268	.0262	.0256	.0250	.0244	.0239	.0233
-1.8	.0359	.0351	.0344	.0336	.0329	.0322	.0314	.0307	.0301	.0294
-1.7	.0446	.0436	.0427	.0418	.0409	.0401	.0392	.0384	.0375	.0367
-1.6	.0548	.0537	.0526	.0516	.0505	.0495	.0485	.0475	.0465	.0455
-1.5	.0668	.0655	.0643	.0630	.0618	.0606	.0594	.0582	.0571	.0559
-1.4	.0808	.0793	.0778	.0764	.0749	.0735	.0721	.0708	.0694	.0681
-1.3	.0968	.0951	.0934	.0918	.0901	.0885	.0869	.0853	.0838	.0823
-1.2	.1151	.1131	.1112	.1093	.1075	.1056	.1038	.1020	.1003	.0985
-1.1	.1357	.1335	.1314	.1292	.1271	.1251	.1230	.1210	.1190	.1170
-1.0	.1587	.1562	.1539	.1515	.1492	.1469	.1446	.1423	.1401	.1379
-0.9	.1841	.1814	.1788	.1762	.1736	.1711	.1685	.1660	.1635	.1611
-0.8	.2119	.2090	.2061	.2033	.2005	.1977	.1949	.1922	.1894	.1867
-0.7	.2420	.2389	.2358	.2327	.2296	.2266	.2236	.2206	.2177	.2148
-0.6	.2743	.2709	.2676	.2643	.2611	.2578	.2546	.2514	.2483	.2451
-0.5	.3085	.3050	.3015	.2981	.2946	.2912	.2877	.2843	.2810	.2776
-0.4	.3446	.3409	.3372	.3336	.3300	.3264	.3228	.3192	.3156	.3121
-0.3	.3821	.3783	.3745	.3707	.3669	.3632	.3594	.3557	.3520	.3483
-0.2	.4207	.4168	.4129	.4090	.4052	.4013	.3974	.3936	.3897	.3859
-0.1	.4602	.4562	.4522	.4483	.4443	.4404	.4364	.4325	.4286	.4247
-0.0	.5000	.4960	.4920	.4880	.4840	.4801	.4761	.4721	.4681	.4641
0.0	.5000	.5040	.5080	.5120	.5160	.5199	.5239	.5279	.5319	.5359
0.1	.5398	.5438	.5478	.5517	.5557	.5596	.5636	.5675	.5714	.5753
0.2	.5793	.5832	.5871	.5910	.5948	.5987	.6026	.6064	.6103	.6141
0.3	.6179	.6217	.6255	.6293	.6331	.6368	.6406	.6443	.6480	.6517

z	.00	.01	.02	.03	.04	.05	.06	.07	.08	.09
0.4	.6554	.6591	.6628	.6664	.6700	.6736	.6772	.6808	.6844	.6879
0.5	.6915	.6950	.6985	.7019	.7054	.7088	.7123	.7157	.7190	.7224
0.6	.7257	.7291	.7324	.7357	.7389	.7422	.7454	.7486	.7517	.7549
0.7	.7580	.7611	.7642	.7673	.7704	.7734	.7764	.7794	.7823	.7852
0.8	.7881	.7910	.7939	.7967	.7995	.8023	.8051	.8078	.8106	.8133
0.9	.8159	.8186	.8212	.8238	.8264	.8289	.8315	.8340	.8365	.8389
1.0	.8413	.8438	.8461	.8485	.8508	.8531	.8554	.8577	.8599	.8621
1.1	.8643	.8665	.8686	.8708	.8729	.8749	.8770	.8790	.8810	.8830
1.2	.8849	.8869	.8888	.8907	.8925	.8944	.8962	.8980	.8997	.9015
1.3	.9032	.9049	.9066	.9082	.9099	.9115	.9131	.9147	.9162	.9177
1.4	.9192	.9207	.9222	.9236	.9251	.9265	.9279	.9292	.9306	.9319
1.5	.9332	.9345	.9357	.9370	.9382	.9394	.9406	.9418	.9429	.9441
1.6	.9452	.9463	.9474	.9484	.9495	.9505	.9515	.9525	.9535	.9545
1.7	.9554	.9564	.9573	.9582	.9591	.9599	.9608	.9616	.9625	.9633
1.8	.9641	.9649	.9656	.9664	.9671	.9678	.9686	.9693	.9699	.9706
1.9	.9713	.9719	.9726	.9732	.9738	.9744	.9750	.9756	.9761	.9767
2.0	.9772	.9778	.9783	.9788	.9793	.9798	.9803	.9808	.9812	.9817
2.1	.9821	.9826	.9830	.9834	.9838	.9842	.9846	.9850	.9854	.9857
2.2	.9861	.9864	.9868	.9871	.9875	.9878	.9881	.9884	.9887	.9890
2.3	.9893	.9896	.9898	.9901	.9904	.9906	.9909	.9911	.9913	.9916
2.4	.9918	.9920	.9922	.9925	.9927	.9929	.9931	.9932	.9934	.9936
2.5	.9938	.9940	.9941	.9943	.9945	.9946	.9948	.9949	.9951	.9952
2.6	.9953	.9955	.9956	.9957	.9959	.9960	.9961	.9962	.9963	.9964
2.7	.9965	.9966	.9967	.9968	.9969	.9970	.9971	.9972	.9973	.9974
2.8	.9974	.9975	.9976	.9977	.9977	.9978	.9979	.9979	.9980	.9981
2.9	.9981	.9982	.9982	.9983	.9984	.9984	.9985	.9985	.9986	.9986
3.0	.9987	.9987	.9987	.9988	.9988	.9989	.9989	.9989	.9990	.9990
3.1	.9990	.9991	.9991	.9991	.9992	.9992	.9992	.9992	.9993	.9993
3.2	.9993	.9993	.9994	.9994	.9994	.9994	.9994	.9995	.9995	.9995
3.3	.9995	.9995	.9995	.9996	.9996	.9996	.9996	.9996	.9996	.9997
3.4	.9997	.9997	.9997	.9997	.9997	.9997	.9997	.9997	.9997	.9998
3.5	.9998	.9998	.9998	.9998	.9998	.9998	.9998	.9998	.9998	.9998
3.6	.9998	.9998	.9999	.9999	.9999	.9999	.9999	.9999	.9999	.9999
3.7	.9999	.9999	.9999	.9999	.9999	.9999	.9999	.9999	.9999	.9999
3.8	.9999	.9999	.9999	.9999	.9999	.9999	.9999	.9999	.9999	.9999

Source: The cumulative normal probablilities were generated in Excel.

Student's *t*-Distribution

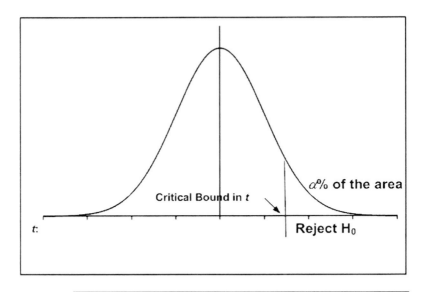

$\alpha =$		0.10	0.05	0.025	0.01	0.005
$df =$	1	3.078	6.314	12.706	31.821	63.657
	2	1.886	2.920	4.303	6.965	9.925
	3	1.638	2.353	3.182	4.541	5.841
	4	1.533	2.132	2.776	3.747	4.604
	5	1.476	2.015	2.571	3.365	4.032
	6	1.440	1.943	2.447	3.143	3.707
	7	1.415	1.895	2.365	2.998	3.499
	8	1.397	1.860	2.306	2.896	3.355
	9	1.383	1.833	2.262	2.821	3.250
	10	1.372	1.812	2.228	2.764	3.169
	11	1.363	1.796	2.201	2.718	3.106
	12	1.356	1.782	2.179	2.681	3.055
	13	1.350	1.771	2.160	2.650	3.012
	14	1.345	1.761	2.145	2.624	2.977
	15	1.341	1.753	2.131	2.602	2.947
	16	1.337	1.746	2.120	2.583	2.921
	17	1.333	1.740	2.110	2.567	2.898
	18	1.330	1.734	2.101	2.552	2.878

$\alpha =$	0.10	0.05	0.025	0.01	0.005
19	1.328	1.729	2.093	2.539	2.861
20	1.325	1.725	2.086	2.528	2.845
21	1.323	1.721	2.080	2.518	2.831
22	1.321	1.717	2.074	2.508	2.819
23	1.319	1.714	2.069	2.500	2.807
24	1.318	1.711	2.064	2.492	2.797
25	1.316	1.708	2.060	2.485	2.787
26	1.315	1.706	2.056	2.479	2.779
27	1.314	1.703	2.052	2.473	2.771
28	1.313	1.701	2.048	2.467	2.763
29	1.311	1.699	2.045	2.462	2.756
30	1.310	1.697	2.042	2.457	2.750
31	1.309	1.696	2.040	2.453	2.744
32	1.309	1.694	2.037	2.449	2.738
33	1.308	1.692	2.035	2.445	2.733
34	1.307	1.691	2.032	2.441	2.728
35	1.306	1.690	2.030	2.438	2.724
36	1.306	1.688	2.028	2.434	2.719
37	1.305	1.687	2.026	2.431	2.715
38	1.304	1.686	2.024	2.429	2.712
39	1.304	1.685	2.023	2.426	2.708
40	1.303	1.684	2.021	2.423	2.704
41	1.303	1.683	2.020	2.421	2.701
42	1.302	1.682	2.018	2.418	2.698
43	1.302	1.681	2.017	2.416	2.695
44	1.301	1.680	2.015	2.414	2.692
45	1.301	1.679	2.014	2.412	2.690
46	1.300	1.679	2.013	2.410	2.687
47	1.300	1.678	2.012	2.408	2.685
48	1.299	1.677	2.011	2.407	2.682
49	1.299	1.677	2.010	2.405	2.680
50	1.299	1.676	2.009	2.403	2.678
51	1.298	1.675	2.008	2.402	2.676
52	1.298	1.675	2.007	2.400	2.674
53	1.298	1.674	2.006	2.399	2.672

$\alpha =$	0.10	0.05	0.025	0.01	0.005
54	1.297	1.674	2.005	2.397	2.670
55	1.297	1.673	2.004	2.396	2.668
56	1.297	1.673	2.003	2.395	2.667
57	1.297	1.672	2.002	2.394	2.665
58	1.296	1.672	2.002	2.392	2.663
59	1.296	1.671	2.001	2.391	2.662
60	1.296	1.671	2.000	2.390	2.660
61	1.296	1.670	2.000	2.389	2.659
62	1.295	1.670	1.999	2.388	2.657
63	1.295	1.669	1.998	2.387	2.656
64	1.295	1.669	1.998	2.386	2.655
65	1.295	1.669	1.997	2.385	2.654
66	1.295	1.668	1.997	2.384	2.652
67	1.294	1.668	1.996	2.383	2.651
68	1.294	1.668	1.995	2.382	2.650
69	1.294	1.667	1.995	2.382	2.649
70	1.294	1.667	1.994	2.381	2.648
71	1.294	1.667	1.994	2.380	2.647
72	1.293	1.666	1.993	2.379	2.646
73	1.293	1.666	1.993	2.379	2.645
74	1.293	1.666	1.993	2.378	2.644
75	1.293	1.665	1.992	2.377	2.643
76	1.293	1.665	1.992	2.376	2.642
77	1.293	1.665	1.991	2.376	2.641
78	1.292	1.665	1.991	2.375	2.640

$a =$	0.10	0.05	0.025	0.01	0.005
79	1.292	1.664	1.990	2.374	2.640
80	1.292	1.664	1.990	2.374	2.639
81	1.292	1.664	1.990	2.373	2.638
82	1.292	1.664	1.989	2.373	2.637
83	1.292	1.663	1.989	2.372	2.636
84	1.292	1.663	1.989	2.372	2.636
85	1.292	1.663	1.988	2.371	2.635
86	1.291	1.663	1.988	2.370	2.634
87	1.291	1.663	1.988	2.370	2.634
88	1.291	1.662	1.987	2.369	2.633
89	1.291	1.662	1.987	2.369	2.632
90	1.291	1.662	1.987	2.368	2.632
91	1.291	1.662	1.986	2.368	2.631
92	1.291	1.662	1.986	2.368	2.630
93	1.291	1.661	1.986	2.367	2.630
94	1.291	1.661	1.986	2.367	2.629
95	1.291	1.661	1.985	2.366	2.629
96	1.290	1.661	1.985	2.366	2.628
97	1.290	1.661	1.985	2.365	2.627
98	1.290	1.661	1.984	2.365	2.627
99	1.290	1.660	1.984	2.365	2.626
100	1.290	1.660	1.984	2.364	2.626
120	1.289	1.658	1.980	2.358	2.617
∞	1.282	1.645	1.96	2.326	2.576

Source: The *t*-coefficients were generated in Excel.

F Tables

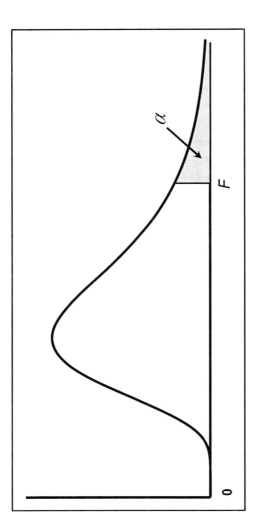

Each of the following *F*-Tables contains the value for the upper boundary of the *F*-distribution for a given numerator and denominator degree of freedom that marks off 0.10, 0.05, 0.025, and 0.01 of the area in the tail of the distribution.

F Table, $\alpha = 0.10$

denom df	num df																			
	1	2	3	4	5	6	7	8	9	10	12	15	20	24	30	40	60	120	∞
1	39.86	49.50	53.59	55.83	57.24	58.20	58.91	59.44	59.86	60.19	60.71	61.22	61.74	62.00	62.26	62.53	62.79	63.06	63.33
2	8.53	9.00	9.16	9.24	9.29	9.33	9.35	9.37	9.38	9.39	9.41	9.42	9.44	9.45	9.46	9.47	9.47	9.48	9.49
3	5.54	5.46	5.39	5.34	5.31	5.28	5.27	5.25	5.24	5.23	5.22	5.20	5.18	5.18	5.17	5.16	5.15	5.14	5.13
4	4.54	4.32	4.19	4.11	4.05	4.01	3.98	3.95	3.94	3.92	3.90	3.87	3.84	3.83	3.82	3.80	3.79	3.78	3.76
5	4.06	3.78	3.62	3.52	3.45	3.40	3.37	3.34	3.32	3.30	3.27	3.24	3.21	3.19	3.17	3.16	3.14	3.12	3.10
6	3.78	3.46	3.29	3.18	3.11	3.05	3.01	2.98	2.96	2.94	2.90	2.87	2.84	2.82	2.80	2.78	2.76	2.74	2.72
7	3.59	3.26	3.07	2.96	2.88	2.83	2.78	2.75	2.72	2.70	2.67	2.63	2.59	2.58	2.56	2.54	2.51	2.49	2.47
8	3.46	3.11	2.92	2.81	2.73	2.67	2.62	2.59	2.56	2.54	2.50	2.46	2.42	2.40	2.38	2.36	2.34	2.32	2.29
9	3.36	3.01	2.81	2.69	2.61	2.55	2.51	2.47	2.44	2.42	2.38	2.34	2.30	2.28	2.25	2.23	2.21	2.18	2.16
10	3.29	2.92	2.73	2.61	2.52	2.46	2.41	2.38	2.35	2.32	2.28	2.24	2.20	2.18	2.16	2.13	2.11	2.08	2.06
12	3.18	2.81	2.61	2.48	2.39	2.33	2.28	2.24	2.21	2.19	2.15	2.10	2.06	2.04	2.01	1.99	1.96	1.93	1.90
15	3.07	2.70	2.49	2.36	2.27	2.21	2.16	2.12	2.09	2.06	2.02	1.97	1.92	1.90	1.87	1.85	1.82	1.79	1.76
20	2.97	2.59	2.38	2.25	2.16	2.09	2.04	2.00	1.96	1.94	1.89	1.84	1.79	1.77	1.74	1.71	1.68	1.64	1.61
24	2.93	2.54	2.33	2.19	2.10	2.04	1.98	1.94	1.91	1.88	1.83	1.78	1.73	1.70	1.67	1.64	1.61	1.57	1.53
30	2.88	2.49	2.28	2.14	2.05	1.98	1.93	1.88	1.85	1.82	1.77	1.72	1.67	1.64	1.61	1.57	1.54	1.50	1.46
40	2.84	2.44	2.23	2.09	2.00	1.93	1.87	1.83	1.79	1.76	1.71	1.66	1.61	1.57	1.54	1.51	1.47	1.42	1.38
60	2.79	2.39	2.18	2.04	1.95	1.87	1.82	1.77	1.74	1.71	1.66	1.60	1.54	1.51	1.48	1.44	1.40	1.35	1.29
120	2.75	2.35	2.13	1.99	1.90	1.82	1.77	1.72	1.68	1.65	1.60	1.55	1.48	1.45	1.41	1.37	1.32	1.26	1.19
∞	2.71	2.30	2.08	1.94	1.85	1.77	1.72	1.67	1.63	1.60	1.55	1.49	1.42	1.38	1.34	1.30	1.24	1.17	1.00

F Table, $\alpha = 0.05$

denom df	num df																		
	1	2	3	4	5	6	7	8	9	10	12	15	20	24	30	40	60	120	∞
1	161.4	199.5	215.7	224.6	230.2	234.0	236.8	238.9	240.5	241.9	243.9	245.9	248.0	249.1	250.1	251.1	252.2	253.3	254.3
2	18.51	19.00	19.16	19.25	19.30	19.33	19.35	19.37	19.38	19.40	19.41	19.43	19.45	19.45	19.46	19.47	19.48	19.49	19.50
3	10.13	9.55	9.28	9.12	9.01	8.94	8.89	8.85	8.81	8.79	8.74	8.70	8.66	8.64	8.62	8.59	8.57	8.55	8.53
4	7.71	6.94	6.59	6.39	6.26	6.16	6.09	6.04	6.00	5.96	5.91	5.86	5.80	5.77	5.75	5.72	5.69	5.66	5.63
5	6.61	5.79	5.41	5.19	5.05	4.95	4.88	4.82	4.77	4.74	4.68	4.62	4.56	4.53	4.50	4.46	4.43	4.40	4.36
6	5.99	5.14	4.76	4.53	4.39	4.28	4.21	4.15	4.10	4.06	4.00	3.94	3.87	3.84	3.81	3.77	3.74	3.70	3.67
7	5.59	4.74	4.35	4.12	3.97	3.87	3.79	3.73	3.68	3.64	3.57	3.51	3.44	3.41	3.38	3.34	3.30	3.27	3.23
8	5.32	4.46	4.07	3.84	3.69	3.58	3.50	3.44	3.39	3.35	3.28	3.22	3.15	3.12	3.08	3.04	3.01	2.97	2.93
9	5.12	4.26	3.86	3.63	3.48	3.37	3.29	3.23	3.18	3.14	3.07	3.01	2.94	2.90	2.86	2.83	2.79	2.75	2.71
10	4.96	4.10	3.71	3.48	3.33	3.22	3.14	3.07	3.02	2.98	2.91	2.85	2.77	2.74	2.70	2.66	2.62	2.58	2.54
12	4.75	3.89	3.49	3.26	3.11	3.00	2.91	2.85	2.80	2.75	2.69	2.62	2.54	2.51	2.47	2.43	2.38	2.34	2.30
15	4.54	3.68	3.29	3.06	2.90	2.79	2.71	2.64	2.59	2.54	2.48	2.40	2.33	2.29	2.25	2.20	2.16	2.11	2.07
20	4.35	3.49	3.10	2.87	2.71	2.60	2.51	2.45	2.39	2.35	2.28	2.20	2.12	2.08	2.04	1.99	1.95	1.90	1.84
24	4.26	3.40	3.01	2.78	2.62	2.51	2.42	2.36	2.30	2.25	2.18	2.11	2.03	1.98	1.94	1.89	1.84	1.79	1.73
30	4.17	3.32	2.92	2.69	2.53	2.42	2.33	2.27	2.21	2.16	2.09	2.01	1.93	1.89	1.84	1.79	1.74	1.68	1.62
40	4.08	3.23	2.84	2.61	2.45	2.34	2.25	2.18	2.12	2.08	2.00	1.92	1.84	1.79	1.74	1.69	1.64	1.58	1.51
60	4.00	3.15	2.76	2.53	2.37	2.25	2.17	2.10	2.04	1.99	1.92	1.84	1.75	1.70	1.65	1.59	1.53	1.47	1.39
120	3.92	3.07	2.68	2.45	2.29	2.18	2.09	2.02	1.96	1.91	1.83	1.75	1.66	1.61	1.55	1.50	1.43	1.35	1.25
∞	3.84	3.00	2.60	2.37	2.21	2.10	2.01	1.94	1.88	1.83	1.75	1.67	1.57	1.52	1.46	1.39	1.32	1.22	1.00

F Table, α = 0.025

denom df	num df																		
	1	2	3	4	5	6	7	8	9	10	12	15	20	24	30	40	60	120	∞
1	647.8	799.5	864.2	899.6	921.8	937.1	948.2	956.7	963.3	968.6	976.7	984.9	993.1	997.2	1001	1006	1010	1014	1018
2	38.51	39.00	39.17	39.25	39.30	39.33	39.36	39.37	39.39	39.40	39.41	39.43	39.45	39.46	39.46	39.47	39.48	39.49	39.50
3	17.44	16.04	15.44	15.10	14.88	14.73	14.62	14.54	14.47	14.42	14.34	14.25	14.17	14.12	14.08	14.04	13.99	13.95	13.90
4	12.22	10.65	9.98	9.60	9.36	9.20	9.07	8.98	8.90	8.84	8.75	8.66	8.56	8.51	8.46	8.41	8.36	8.31	8.26
5	10.01	8.43	7.76	7.39	7.15	6.98	6.85	6.76	6.68	6.62	6.52	6.43	6.33	6.28	6.23	6.18	6.12	6.07	6.02
6	8.81	7.26	6.60	6.23	5.99	5.82	5.70	5.60	5.52	5.46	5.37	5.27	5.17	5.12	5.07	5.01	4.96	4.90	4.85
7	8.07	6.54	5.89	5.52	5.29	5.12	4.99	4.90	4.82	4.76	4.67	4.57	4.47	4.41	4.36	4.31	4.25	4.20	4.14
8	7.57	6.06	5.42	5.05	4.82	4.65	4.53	4.43	4.36	4.30	4.20	4.10	4.00	3.95	3.89	3.84	3.78	3.73	3.67
9	7.21	5.71	5.08	4.72	4.48	4.32	4.20	4.10	4.03	3.96	3.87	3.77	3.67	3.61	3.56	3.51	3.45	3.39	3.33
10	6.94	5.46	4.83	4.47	4.24	4.07	3.95	3.85	3.78	3.72	3.62	3.52	3.42	3.37	3.31	3.26	3.20	3.14	3.08
12	6.55	5.10	4.47	4.12	3.89	3.73	3.61	3.51	3.44	3.37	3.28	3.18	3.07	3.02	2.96	2.91	2.85	2.79	2.72
15	6.20	4.77	4.15	3.80	3.58	3.41	3.29	3.20	3.12	3.06	2.96	2.86	2.76	2.70	2.64	2.59	2.52	2.46	2.40
20	5.87	4.46	3.86	3.51	3.29	3.13	3.01	2.91	2.84	2.77	2.68	2.57	2.46	2.41	2.35	2.29	2.22	2.16	2.09
24	5.72	4.32	3.72	3.38	3.15	2.99	2.87	2.78	2.70	2.64	2.54	2.44	2.33	2.27	2.21	2.15	2.08	2.01	1.94
30	5.57	4.18	3.59	3.25	3.03	2.87	2.75	2.65	2.57	2.51	2.41	2.31	2.20	2.14	2.07	2.01	1.94	1.87	1.79
40	5.42	4.05	3.46	3.13	2.90	2.74	2.62	2.53	2.45	2.39	2.29	2.18	2.07	2.01	1.94	1.88	1.80	1.72	1.64
60	5.29	3.93	3.34	3.01	2.79	2.63	2.51	2.41	2.33	2.27	2.17	2.06	1.94	1.88	1.82	1.74	1.67	1.58	1.48
120	5.15	3.80	3.23	2.89	2.67	2.52	2.39	2.30	2.22	2.16	2.05	1.94	1.82	1.76	1.69	1.61	1.53	1.43	1.31
∞	5.02	3.69	3.12	2.79	2.57	2.41	2.29	2.19	2.11	2.05	1.94	1.83	1.71	1.64	1.57	1.48	1.39	1.27	1.00

F Table, α = 0.01

denom df	num df 1	2	3	4	5	6	7	8	9	10	12	15	20	24	30	40	60	120	∞
1	4052	5000	5403	5625	5764	5859	5928	5981	6022	6056	6106	6157	6209	6235	6261	6287	6313	6339	6366
2	98.50	99.00	99.17	99.25	99.30	99.33	99.36	99.37	99.39	99.40	99.42	99.43	99.45	99.46	99.47	99.47	99.48	99.49	99.50
3	34.12	30.82	29.46	28.71	28.24	27.91	27.67	27.49	27.35	27.23	27.05	26.87	26.69	26.60	26.50	26.41	26.32	26.22	26.13
4	21.20	18.00	16.69	15.98	15.52	15.21	14.98	14.80	14.66	14.55	14.37	14.20	14.02	13.93	13.84	13.75	13.65	13.56	13.46
5	16.26	13.27	12.06	11.39	10.97	10.67	10.46	10.29	10.16	10.05	9.89	9.72	9.55	9.47	9.38	9.29	9.20	9.11	9.02
6	13.75	10.92	9.78	9.15	8.75	8.47	8.26	8.10	7.98	7.87	7.72	7.56	7.40	7.31	7.23	7.14	7.06	6.97	6.88
7	12.25	9.55	8.45	7.85	7.46	7.19	6.99	6.84	6.72	6.62	6.47	6.31	6.16	6.07	5.99	5.91	5.82	5.74	5.65
8	11.26	8.65	7.59	7.01	6.63	6.37	6.18	6.03	5.91	5.81	5.67	5.52	5.36	5.28	5.20	5.12	5.03	4.95	4.86
9	10.56	8.02	6.99	6.42	6.06	5.80	5.61	5.47	5.35	5.26	5.11	4.96	4.81	4.73	4.65	4.57	4.48	4.40	4.31
10	10.04	7.56	6.55	5.99	5.64	5.39	5.20	5.06	4.94	4.85	4.71	4.56	4.41	4.33	4.25	4.17	4.08	4.00	3.91
12	9.33	6.93	5.95	5.41	5.06	4.82	4.64	4.50	4.39	4.30	4.16	4.01	3.86	3.78	3.70	3.62	3.54	3.45	3.36
15	8.68	6.36	5.42	4.89	4.56	4.32	4.14	4.00	3.89	3.80	3.67	3.52	3.37	3.29	3.21	3.13	3.05	2.96	2.87
20	8.10	5.85	4.94	4.43	4.10	3.87	3.70	3.56	3.46	3.37	3.23	3.09	2.94	2.86	2.78	2.69	2.61	2.52	2.42
24	7.82	5.61	4.72	4.22	3.90	3.67	3.50	3.36	3.26	3.17	3.03	2.89	2.74	2.66	2.58	2.49	2.40	2.31	2.21
30	7.56	5.39	4.51	4.02	3.70	3.47	3.30	3.17	3.07	2.98	2.84	2.70	2.55	2.47	2.39	2.30	2.21	2.11	2.01
40	7.31	5.18	4.31	3.83	3.51	3.29	3.12	2.99	2.89	2.80	2.66	2.52	2.37	2.29	2.20	2.11	2.02	1.92	1.80
60	7.08	4.98	4.13	3.65	3.34	3.12	2.95	2.82	2.72	2.63	2.50	2.35	2.20	2.12	2.03	1.94	1.84	1.66	1.60
120	6.85	4.79	3.95	3.48	3.17	2.96	2.79	2.66	2.56	2.47	2.34	2.19	2.03	1.95	1.86	1.76	1.66	1.53	1.38
∞	6.63	4.61	3.78	3.32	3.02	2.80	2.64	2.51	2.41	2.32	2.18	2.04	1.88	1.79	1.70	1.59	1.47	1.32	1.00

Chi-Square Table

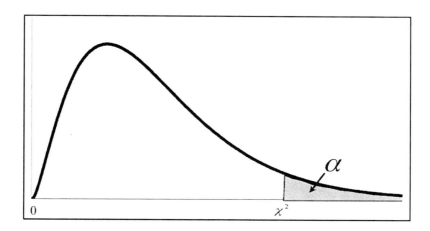

df	0.10	0.05	0.025	0.01	0.005
1	2.706	3.841	5.024	6.635	7.879
2	4.605	5.991	7.378	9.210	10.597
3	6.251	7.815	9.348	11.345	12.838
4	7.779	9.488	11.143	13.277	14.860
5	9.236	11.070	12.833	15.086	16.750
6	10.645	12.592	14.449	16.812	18.548
7	12.017	14.067	16.013	18.475	20.278
8	13.362	15.507	17.535	20.090	21.955
9	14.684	16.919	19.023	21.666	23.589
10	15.987	18.307	20.483	23.209	25.188
11	17.275	19.675	21.920	24.725	26.757
12	18.549	21.026	23.337	26.217	28.300
13	19.812	22.362	24.736	27.688	29.819
14	21.064	23.685	26.119	29.141	31.319
15	22.307	24.996	27.488	30.578	32.801
16	23.542	26.296	28.845	32.000	34.267
17	24.769	27.587	30.191	33.409	35.718
18	25.989	28.869	31.526	34.805	37.156
19	27.204	30.144	32.852	36.191	38.582
20	28.412	31.410	34.170	37.566	39.997

df	0.10	0.05	0.025	0.01	0.005
21	29.615	32.671	35.479	38.932	41.401
22	30.813	33.924	36.781	40.289	42.796
23	32.007	35.172	38.076	41.638	44.181
24	33.196	36.415	39.364	42.980	45.559
25	34.382	37.652	40.646	44.314	46.928
26	35.563	38.885	41.923	45.642	48.290
27	36.741	40.113	43.195	46.963	49.645
28	37.916	41.337	44.461	48.278	50.993
29	39.087	42.557	45.722	49.588	52.336
30	40.256	43.773	46.979	50.892	53.672
31	41.422	44.985	48.232	52.191	55.003
32	42.585	46.194	49.480	53.486	56.328
33	43.745	47.400	50.725	54.776	57.648
34	44.903	48.602	51.966	56.061	58.964
35	46.059	49.802	53.203	57.342	60.275
36	47.212	50.998	54.437	58.619	61.581
37	48.363	52.192	55.668	59.893	62.883
38	49.513	53.384	56.896	61.162	64.181
39	50.660	54.572	58.120	62.428	65.476
40	51.805	55.758	59.342	63.691	66.766
41	52.949	56.942	60.561	64.950	68.053
42	54.090	58.124	61.777	66.206	69.336
43	55.230	59.304	62.990	67.459	70.616
44	56.369	60.481	64.201	68.710	71.893
45	57.505	61.656	65.410	69.957	73.166
46	58.641	62.830	66.617	71.201	74.437
47	59.774	64.001	67.821	72.443	75.704
48	60.907	65.171	69.023	73.683	76.969
49	62.038	66.339	70.222	74.919	78.231
50	63.167	67.505	71.420	76.154	79.490
60	74.397	79.082	83.298	88.379	91.952
70	85.527	90.531	95.023	100.425	104.215
80	96.578	101.879	106.629	112.329	116.321
90	107.565	113.145	118.136	124.116	128.299
100	118.498	124.342	129.561	135.807	140.169

Index

Note: The *f* and *t* following page numbers refer to figures and tables, respectively.

Announcing the Business Expert Press Digital Library

*Concise E-books Business Students
Need for Classroom and Research*

This book can also be purchased in an e-book collection by your library as

- a one-time purchase,
- that is owned forever,
- allows for simultaneous readers,
- has no restrictions on printing,
- can be downloaded as PDFs from within the library community.

Our digital library collections are a great solution to beat the rising cost of textbooks. E-books can be loaded into their course management systems or onto students' e-book readers.

The **Business Expert Press** digital libraries are very affordable, with no obligation to buy in future years.

For more information, please visit www.**businessexpertpress.com/librarians**. To set up a trial in the United States, please contact **Sheri Allen** at *sheri.allen@globalepress.com*; for all other regions, contact **Nicole Lee** at *nicole.lee@igroupnet.com*.

OTHER TITLES IN OUR QUANTITATIVE APPROACHES TO DECISION MAKING COLLECTION

CPSIA information can be obtained at www.ICGtesting.com
Printed in the USA
BVOW030018210212

283381BV00006B/7/P